Lecture Notes in Computer Science 8406

Commenced Publication in 1973
Founding and Former Series Editors:
Gerhard Goos, Juris Hartmanis, and Jan van Leeuwen

Alberto Dainotti   Anirban Mahanti
Steve Uhlig (Eds.)

Traffic Monitoring and Analysis

6th International Workshop, TMA 2014
London, UK, April 14, 2014
Proceedings

 Springer

Volume Editors

Alberto Dainotti
University of California, San Diego Supercomputer Center
9500 Gilman Drive, MC 0505, La Jolla, CA 92093-0505, USA
E-mail: alberto@caida.org

Anirban Mahanti
NICTA, Networks Research Group
13 Garden Street, Eveleigh, NSW 2015, Australia
E-mail: anirban.mahanti@nicta.com.au

Steve Uhlig
Queen Mary, University of London
School of Electronic Engineering and Computer Science
Mile End Road, London E1 4NS, UK
E-mail: steve.uhlig@qmul.ac.uk

ISSN 0302-9743   e-ISSN 1611-3349
ISBN 978-3-642-54998-4   e-ISBN 978-3-642-54999-1
DOI 10.1007/978-3-642-54999-1
Springer Heidelberg New York Dordrecht London

Library of Congress Control Number: 2014935158

LNCS Sublibrary: SL 5 – Computer Communication Networks
and Telecommunications

Typesetting: Camera-ready by author, data conversion by Scientific Publishing Services, Chennai, India

Printed on acid-free paper

Springer is part of Springer Science+Business Media (www.springer.com)

Message from the Program Co-Chairs

The sixth Traffic Monitoring and Analysis (TMA) workshop took place in London, UK. TMA continues its focus on novel aspects of network measurements and traffic monitoring research, as well as on validation (or invalidation) of previous work.

The technical program includes papers on a wide range of topics in network measurements, including tools, performance analysis, the Web, content delivery, and inter-domain routing. This year TMA received 30 submissions, with authors from both academia and industry.

The program was the result of a thorough two-staged review process. In the first stage, papers were assigned to Technical Program Committee (TPC) members for review. The TPC consisted of 37 researchers, with expertise covering the topics of interest to TMA, and were drawn from academic and industrial institutes around the world. The TPC worked diligently, writing many thoughtful, fair, and thorough reviews. Most papers had received three reviews by the end of this stage. As chairs, we read through the reviews, comments, and considered the final scores to arrive at a preliminary categorization of the papers. Subsequently, we proceeded to online deliberations of the papers and the reviews. There was no explicit cap on the number of papers to be accepted. Our brief to the TPC was to arrive at "consensus" decisions through discussions and accept all "qualified" papers. Where necessary, we sought additional reviews during the discussion phase. The TPC, along with external experts, wrote 116 reviews and exchanged close to 145 comments. The TPC considered technical quality, originality, and relevance to the workshop and recommended accepting 11 full papers. All accepted papers were assigned a shepherd to ensure that the authors had addressed the reviewers' comments adequately.

Throughout the review process, special attention was paid to conflicts, and in particular to papers conflicting with the TPC chairs. These were not visible to them in the submission management system. Papers conflict with TPC members were marked in the conference management system and were reviewed only by non-conflict TPC members.

The final program is the result of the hard work of many individuals. We thank all the authors who submitted their work to TMA. We appreciate the effort that goes into producing a quality research paper and hope that authors received useful feedback on their submissions. As program chairs, we would like to extend a big thank you to our hardworking TPC members for volunteering their time and expertise with passion.

This is a special year for TMA, since this is the first edition of the workshop not co-located with another conference. Nevertheless, there was significant interest and involvement both from authors and TPC members, resulting in a high quality program.

Thank you all for attending the workshop. We hope you enjoyed the program.

February 2014

Alberto Dainotti
Anirban Mahanti
Steve Uhlig

Organization

Executive Committee

Workshop Chairs

Alberto Dainotti	CAIDA, UC San Diego, USA
Anirban Mahanti	NICTA, Australia
Steve Uhlig	Queen Mary University of London, UK

Steering Committee

Ernst Biersack	EURECOM, France
Xenofontas Dimitropoulos	University of Crete/FORTH, Greece
Jordi Domingo-Pascual	Universitat Politècnica de Catalunya, Spain
Christian Kreibich	ICSI, USA
Marco Mellia	Politecnico di Torino, Italy
Philippe Owezarski	CNRS, France
Maria Papadopouli	University of Crete, Greece
Konstantina Papagiannaki	Telefónica, Spain
Antonio Pescapè	University of Naples, Italy
Aiko Pras	University of Twente, Netherlands
Fabio Ricciato	Austrian Institute of Technology, Austria
Yuval Shavitt	Tel Aviv University, Israel
Steve Uhlig	Queen Mary University of London, UK

Local Arrangements

Sabri Zaman	Queen Mary University of London, UK
Hamed Saljooghinejad	Queen Mary University of London, UK

Technical Program Committee

Bernhard Ager	ETH Zurich, Switzerland
Theophilus Benson	Princeton, USA
Ernst Biersack	EURECOM, France
Olivier Bonaventure	Université Catholique de Louvain, Belgium
Pedro Casas	FTW, Austria
Kenjiro Cho	IIJ, Japan
Italo Cunha	Universidade Federal de Minas Gerais, Brazil
Alessandro D'Alconzo	FTW, Austria
Amogh Dhamdhere	CAIDA, UC San Diego, USA

Table of Contents

Flow Management at Multi-Gbps: Tradeoffs and Lessons Learned

Georges Nassopulos[1], Dario Rossi[1], Francesco Gringoli[2], Lorenzo Nava[2],
Maurizio Dusi[3], and Pedro Maria Santiago del Rio[4,1]

[1] Telecom ParisTech, Paris, France
[2] Universita' degli Studi di Brescia, Brescia, Italy
[3] NEC Laboratories Europe, Heidelberg, Germany
[4] Universidad Autonoma de Madrid (UAM), Madrid, Spain

Abstract. While the ultimate goal of kernel-level network stacks is to manage individual packets at line rate, the goal of user-level network monitoring applications is instead to match packets with the flow they belong to, and take actions accordingly. With current improvements in Network Interface Cards hardware and network software stacks, traffic monitors and traffic analyzers are fed with multi-Gbps streams of packets – which de facto pushes bottlenecks from kernel-level networking stack up to user-level applications. In this paper, we argue that flow management is a crucial module for any user-application that needs to process traffic at multiple Gbps, and we study the performance impact of different design choices of the flow management module by adopting a trace-driven emulation approach. While our results do not show a single "best" system settings under all circumstances, they highlight several tradeoffs, in terms of, e.g., the kind of structure, its size, and the computational complexity, that may affect system performance in a non-trivial way. We further make our software tools available to the scientific community to promote sharing of best practices.

1 Introduction

As reported by Cisco [1], the Internet traffic has increased more than fourfold over the past five years. Consequently, the processing speed of network devices such as switches and routers, has grown to let devices process incoming packets at line rate, and pass them to user-space processes for carrying out further analysis – such as intrusion detection, flow management, traffic classification and monitoring, accounting, policing, etc.

Two main trends are keys to this evolution. On one hand, modern Network Interface Cards (NICs) hardware can effectively handle packet rates in the order of tens of Gbps. On the other hand, independent approaches have been proposed to overcome the severe software bottlenecks that affect network stacks of standard operating systems (OS). Examples include PF_RING with Threaded NAPI [18] and variants [13], Netmap [27,28], PacketShader [19] and PFQ [11]. These approaches effectively bypass bottlenecks of standard OS stacks, related to the overhead of per-packet operations like buffer allocation and transfer to user-space, by (i) processing multiple packets in batch to limit IRQs and DMA transactions; (ii) exposing memory of packet buffers to the user-space

A. Dainotti, A. Mahanti, and S. Uhlig (Eds.): TMA 2014, LNCS 8406, pp. 1–14, 2014.
© IFIP International Federation for Information Processing 2014

for zero copy access; (iii) tying every capture thread with its own ring buffer to a fixed CPU to increase cache memory hits (Non-Uniform Memory Access) and (iv) using Receive Side Scaling (RSS) to split incoming flows among different input queues/capture threads. Ultimately, these systems pass packets to user space applications, coping with the worst case of small 64Bytes Ethernet frames at 10Gbps per line card.

As a results of these achievements, bottlenecks have been pushed up to user-level applications, which regardless of their ultimate goal –being it classification, intrusion detection, monitoring, policing, etc.– share a common crucial point. Namely, while low-level hardware and drivers manage *packets*, user-level applications manage *flows*. It follows that a primary, general, concern of user-level applications is to correctly and *efficiently* match packets to the corresponding flow, before taking any subsequent action.

Given that it becomes imperative to perform flow management at line-rate, the goal of this paper is to analyze the design space for flow management, which includes comparing different data structures and hashing functions for keeping a table of flows and updating it by adding, searching and removing flows. By analysing the cost of those operations, we aim at shedding light on tradeoffs when performing and implementing effective flow management modules. Note that here we consider the general case where all packets of a flow have to be matched and processed, which for instance relates to traffic classification and intrusion detection systems; we do not consider the load reduction that packet sampling may have on the flow-matching module, as it potentially benefits only a subset of network applications, e.g., traffic characterization and analysis.

This work builds on top of our previous work [31], in which we implement a multi-threaded statistical "early classification" engine (i.e., based on size of the first few packets of a flow [14]) able to cope with several line cards and to classify *real* traffic at 20 Gbps, or 3.2 Mpps, 116 Kfps (and *synthetic* worst case traffic up to 14.2 Mpps and 2.8 Mfps). Yet, as statistical early classification can be done very efficiently [14, 22], one of the main outcome of [31] was to observe that the flow management module represents the system bottleneck, and that higher traffic processing rates would be possible if this bottleneck was removed. Hence, this paper is motivated by the challenge to understand and overcome the flow management bottleneck, sharing knowledge that can hopefully be useful to a greater extent than the narrow classification focus of [31], to improve performance of generic traffic monitoring and analysis tools.

The rest of the paper is organized as follows. In Sec. 2 we motivate and describe the overall system model. In Sec. 3 we describe our methodology, dataset and workflow, from which we gather results reported in Sec. 4. After comparing our work with related effort in Sec. 5, we summarize the main lesson learned and discuss a number of items in our research agenda in Sec. 6.

2   System Model

The system model we consider in this paper builds over the main lessons learned in [31] concerning flow management, that we describe with the help of Fig. 1. In Fig. 1, our multi-thread system sniff packets, placing them in a flow manager structure, that fires classification operations over batches of packets. A traffic analyzer would have a similar structure, with one or more analyzer modules replacing the classification one. Note that,

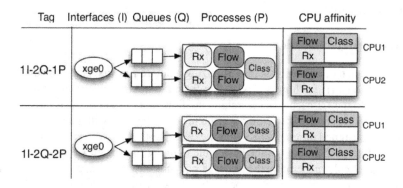

Fig. 1. System model

while the two system configurations in Fig. 1 fire about the same number of threads (represented as shaded block in the rightmost part of Fig. 1, whereas white blocks indicate spare CPU cores), we incurred in severe performance problems (2.1Mpps) whenever two *threads* have concurrently access to the shared flow manager structure (1I-2Q-1P in the figure). Instead, we achieved line rate performance (14.2Mpps) by using two separate *processes*, each of which processed the output of one of the multiple RSS queues exported by the sniffer tools (1I-2Q-2P). Locking issues explain this significant performance gap, and they have to be avoided to allow for sustained system operation [31]. Alternatively, we could avoid locking by replicating the flow manager data structure, letting each thread access a different structure.

Overall, the cost penalty to pay (irrespectively if the solution is mono or multi-process) is a replica of the flow manager data structure to avoid locking. Given a fixed memory budget, it is important to finely tune this structure, as the memory has to be partitioned among multiple independent structures, which are not shared among threads – hence they require no synchronization, or they have no locking issues which reduce the system performance. At the same time, as each structure receives only a portion of the traffic, it may work efficiently with a reduced footprint.

From a more general viewpoint, it would be interesting to optimize flow management operation (as this would possibly lead to extend performance well beyond the 14.2Mpps limit of [31]). Optimization includes not only sizing, but also critical design choices, such as the type of structure (e.g., hash with chaining versus balanced Red-Black trees, etc.) or the choice of the hash function (e.g., CoralReef versus Bob Jenkins, versus Murmur, etc.) that we focus on in this paper.

Otherwise stated, as each process independently receives and analyzes a portion of the whole traffic, we can focus on optimizing an equivalent single-queue single-process system model, as it does not preclude interoperability with recent hardware (e.g., RSS) and software trends early introduced.

3   Methodology

3.1   Trace Driven Emulation

As previously stated, our focus is on optimizing a single pipeline that handles the following operations: (i) fetching a new packet from the queue, which results in loading a new page into the L1 cache, (ii) searching the flow tuple found in the packet into the hash table, which *may* result in either a cache hit or cache miss with page reload.

We hence designed an emulator with an extensible flow tuple feeding interface: to perform the finer grain tuning of the hash table in many significant scenarios we added code for synthetically generating the tuples (e.g., randomly, netscan, portscan, etc.) thus exploring worst case scenarios, and for loading traffic from a trace file. Given that we use backbone traces in the evaluation (whose traffic is notoriously asymmetric), in this work we consider each direction of a traffic flow in isolation for the sake of simplicity. Yet we point out that our results easily extend to bidirectional traffic by XORing source and destination IP addresses and ports before hashing the 5-tuple (which would lead both forward and backward flow directions to be hashed consistently). To evaluate performance of the flow handling code, the emulator loops multiple times over a two step section that stores the tuples into memory first, and then count the time required for matching the tuples into the hash table, eventually adding missing flows, and removing expired ones. While we consider TCP and UDP ports in the flow-matching stage, we do not try to reorder packets by inspecting TCP sequence numbers. As our aim is to focus on general flow-matching performance, we argue that only some applications may require TCP stream reconstruction (e.g., intrusion detection may block subsequent packets of a flow regardless of whether they are received in-order). As such, flow reordering, as for the scope of this work, is left to the spare CPU cores of Fig. 1 and is not performed in what follows.

We release this emulator as an open source software at [2]: with two thousands lines of C code, it embeds both the flow feeding interfaces, the main hash table look-up and the collision managers. About the latter, while the one based on lists pre-allocates directly in the hash table one empty flow element per table line, the one based on the STL RBtree library creates an hash table of tree roots [21]. Clearly this has an impact when chaining is low, as the first flow inside a list is simply copied inside the corresponding empty flow element, while the analogous in the empty tree root requires an initial tree adjustment. Pre-allocating an empty element in the tree without changing the STL library is not possible, that could lead to memory fragmentation issues (see Sec. 6 for future research directions).

While our ultimate goal is to offer insight to fine tune real operational systems such as [31], an experimental approach (i.e., with real traffic over real links) is not suitable for the kind of analysis we carry out in this paper for two main reasons. The first is related to the generality, extensibility and repeatability of our findings. Had we performed tests over the system presented in [31], lessons learned may be of more limited utility for the scientific community. Instead, here we point out that spare CPU cores of Fig. 1 could run any kind of specialized traffic post-process, forwarding, or analysis (whose benchmark is outside the scope of this paper). Second, using the complete network testbed is impractical, and possibly leads to severe bias: indeed, in order to profile each block

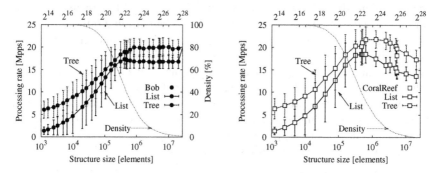

Fig. 2. Structure size tradeoff: Rates of the flow matching process, in Mpps, for different structures and hash functions, as a function of the structure size

to assess the flow matching performance, the system itself was modified introducing a measurement overhead that could impact the performance of the system itself.

As a consequence, in the following we will report our findings only for the trace driven approach. To this purpose, we consider the first 150M packets of the PAIX 2005-01-21 trace from CAIDA [3], collected on a OC48 trunk of an US Commercial Tier1 backbone link connecting San Jose and Seattle.

3.2   Fine Tuning of the Emulation Environment

As a side effect of trace-driven approaches, the data source may run much faster than in the complete experiment, leading to a throughput order of magnitude greater than the original 10Gbps. The reason is two-fold: (i) we store only tuples into memory, packing each packet into a 16 bytes structure, (ii) memory access time is not comparable to the speed of a DMA based system.

While this has no direct impact on the maximum number of flow look up that can be determined *per se*, it makes garbage collection of the hash table critical. If we compute the age of the flows in the hash table using the system clock, the emulation ends up with a greater average occupancy of the table with respect to the network setup (we feed the table with more flows per second while keeping the same time-out age). If otherwise we simulate a time horizon by adding up the delay required to transmit every single packet over a 10Gbps channel (in that case we would have to store each packet length together with the corresponding tuple), we alter the performance evaluation as the flow matching is in real time. For this reason, we opt for using the system clock: while this does not accurately account for performance of the real system, it represents a conservative lower bound of the actual performance (due to higher average occupancy of the data structure with respect to the expected one in real time).

All emulation results are gathered over a 4-cores 3.60 GHz Intel Xeon ES1620 CPU board, equipped with 4x8 GB DIM DDR3 1600Mz RAM memory modules, running Ubuntu 12.04LTS with 64bit Linux kernel version 3.5. As empirical settings of the emulation environment may severely affect the emulation outcomes, we disabled any "smart" feature that dynamically change the rate at which the CPU is working, by (i) disabling hyper-threading features at the BIOS level (ii) fixing CPU frequency governors to `performance` settings, so that CPUs always run at full 3.60 GHz rate (unlike in default `on-demand` configuration that dynamically tunes the CPU frequency settings).

Similarly, we notice that an aggressive caching policy of the Linux kernel severely affects the performance, depending on the data structure being used: e.g., while in case of lists the whole structure is proactively allocated, in case of trees allocations happen on demand, and system caching may impact pages where the memory is allocated. We therefore sync and drop caches (`/proc/sys/vm/drop_caches`) prior to run any emulation to remove bias due to kernel-level memory management policies.

4 Results

We explored over 850 configurations in terms of hash functions, structures types, size settings, and input traffic. Here we report the most interesting trends that we have observed.

We highlight important tradeoffs concerning settings of (i) the structure size, (ii) the algorithmic complexity of the structure management and (iii) the computational complexity of the hash function. These tradeoffs help architectural decisions, and fine tune the flow management module. However, we acknowledge that some of these aspects (e.g., structure size) depends on the input traffic. Hence the proposed tradeoffs point to two main classes of architectures depending on the network scenario envisioned, rather than to a single candidate solution.

Finally, to extend the validity of our findings, we report a sensitivity analysis in terms of (iv) misconfiguration of the flow manager structure and (v) input traffic.

4.1 Structure Size Tradeoff

In Fig. 2, we report the impact of the structure size on system performance, expressed as the packet processing rate, in packet per second. We consider both list (solid line) and trees (dashed line), with either Bob Jenkins [4] (filled circles, left plot) or CoralReef [5] (empty squares, right plot) hashes, varying the structure size from 2^{14} (16K elements) to 2^{28} (268M elements). Left y-axis reports flow matching rate in Mpps (lines with points and confidence interval), whereas right y-axis reports the density of the structure, i.e., the ratio between the used over the total number of rows in the hash table (dotted line, same for lists and trees).

For very small structure sizes, the depth of the tree or the length of the chain dominate the performance, leading to poor flow matching performance. Performance increase nearly logarithmically for both trees and lists (notice the linear slope but the logarithmic x-axis) up to a certain threshold, close to 2^{22} (4M elements) for the CAIDA trace, whose precise value is related to the spatio-temporal traffic mixture.

Extending the structure size beyond the threshold either does not bring any advantage (Bob, left) or even possibly lead to performance penalties (CoralReef, right). In practice, depending on how the structures have been allocated (proactive in case of hash resolving collision by chaining, or reactive in case of trees) pointers can refer to memory areas

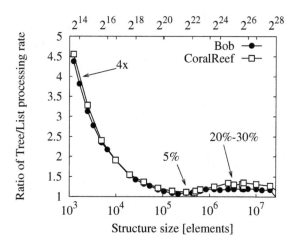

Fig. 3. Structure complexity tradeoff: Ratio between flow matching rates under Trees/Lists

that are stored in different pages, which triggers major page faults and possibly entails quite important performance losses (i.e., about 20% loss in this case for the largest structures).

Otherwise stated, collisions dominate performance of small structures, making the overall throughput low, as expected. Yet, indiscriminately extending the structure size beyond a certain threshold does not necessarily payoff either. Clearly, such over-provisioning situations should be avoided because of bad usage of the allowed memory budget (both Bob and CoralReef cases) and additionally due to possible flow-management performance loss (CoralReef case only). This means that a calibration phase is needed prior to run a tool in a different network environment, or after network upgrade of reconfiguration, and even possibly after traffic mix changes in the same network over longer timeframes.

4.2 Structure Complexity Tradeoff

Fig. 2 also shows another interesting tradeoff that concerns the complexity of algorithmic management. In case of chaining, walking a list of pointers only happens in case of collisions. Conversely, in case of trees more operations have to be done at each element insertion (as the hash points to a memory location containing a pointer toward the root of the tree, implying two memory operations even when the tree has a single element).

Hence, there is an implicit penalty in management of memory pointers in balanced trees, that though often left out of the complexity equation in textbooks, may have an important impact in practice. This can be evinced from Fig. 3 that reports the ratio between flow matching rates under Trees/Lists: it can be gathered that, though a performance improvement exists, it is more significant only in case of improper sizing of the data structures. More particularly: while for very small structures, gain can be up to a factor of 4 and above; for very large structures, gain tops to about than 20-30%; finally,

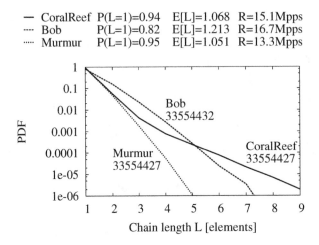

Fig. 4. Computational complexity tradeoff: Chain length probability distribution function (PDF) for CoralReef, Bob and Murmur hash functions

at the critical threshold, gain is about 5%, hinting that proper sizing may play a more important role than structures.

For future work (see Sec. 6), it would be interesting to either consider other data structures (e.g., double hash that avoid chaining), or propose simple tricks to better exploit the simplest data structures (since, as we have seen, performance gain are not necessarily worth the implementation hassle).

4.3 Computational Complexity Tradeoff

Similarly, while different hash functions yield to different amount of collisions, chain length (or, tree depth) explains only part of the story. Indeed, computation of the hash function also consumes resources and impact the flow matching performance.

To highlight this point, we report in Fig. 4 the chain length PDF for the CoralReef, Bob and Murmur hash functions: it can be seen that chains are shorter for Murmur than for Bob or for CoralReef (the latter yielding to longest chains). Yet, notice that the PDF exponentially decreases, which means that the effect of the chain length in case of a properly configured structure size will result in a second order effect.

The figure also reports the probabilities that no chain walking is needed $P(L = 1)$, and the average chain length $E[L]$. Although Murmur hash reduces the collision probability $P(L > 1)$ and average chain length, performance penalty arise in terms of the flow matching rates, due to its implementation complexity[1], which makes it less suitable than simpler CoralReef or Bob hash functions. Hence, in case of Murmur the gain in terms of a lower collision probability and lower chain length are completely offset by the computational complexity needed to achieve it – which makes interesting

---

[1] We are using the murmur implementation offered by authors
http://code.google.com/p/smhasher/.

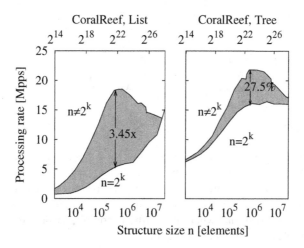

Fig. 5. Misconfiguration of CoralReef structure size

to explore other, faster, alternatives, such as Hsieh hash function [6] or to exploit the pre-computed RSS hash values that are exposed from Intel NICs (see Sec. 6).

4.4 Misconfiguration

As we previously stated, the size of the hash should be tuned according to the workload, as (i) a fixed memory budget must be split among processes running over multiple cores and (ii) performance loss is possible due to unnecessarily large data structures. As such, there is an incentive for researchers and network administrators to finely tune the size of the flow management structure. Problems may raise in case the architecture allows to tune such low level details (e.g., at compile time, or through a configuration file), as careless (or improper) tuning is error prone and can significantly harm the architecture performance.

For instance, while hash functions such as Murmur are inherently robust to the structure size, other hash functions such as CoralReef are not. As we have seen, simpler, computationally faster, hash function such as CoralReef may be preferred in some scenarios. It follows that a tool shipped with a default configuration that is robust for Murmur, may not be robust when the hash function changes. Or, a tool with a default configuration that is robust for CoralReef, may no longer be robust when the structure size is improperly tuned.

Fig. 5 outlines the potential loss for trees and lists. We depict a grey shaded zone between two envelopes: the upper bound is obtained for sizes of the structures that are not powers of two, whereas lower bounds are obtained for powers of two, that are notoriously to avoid in case of CoralReef. The loss in the flow management rate can account to up a factor of 4 in case of lists, and to nearly 30% in case of tree structures. Interestingly, the performance loss is more contained in case of balanced trees, which are inherently more robust to misconfigurations.

Table 1. Bounds to the flow matching rates, CoralReef (54M elements)

	List	Trees
Deterministic	58.1 Mpps	44.6 Mpps
CAIDA	14.6 Mpps	19.7 Mpps
Random	3.1 Mpps	4.6 Mpps

4.5   Input Traffic

While results in the previous section are *qualitative* for general network traffic, *quantitative* performances are bound to the specific trace being used, as well as the hardware capabilities of our emulation environment. Intuitively, flow matching performance can be quantitatively bound between two extreme cases, which are unrealistic as far as the network traffic is concerned: one where the traffic is completely deterministic, vs one where the traffic tuples are completely random.

Interesting observations emerge from Tab. 1. First, as expected real-traffic performance fall in between completely deterministic and completely random 5-tuple sequences. In a sense, this is expected as the entropy of the tuple sequence in the trace is not as high as that of a completely random sequence, since due to temporal scoping of flows, and to heavy hitters, some tuples will be more likely to appear in the sequence. At the same time, skew in the tuple distribution is lower than in the deterministic case, where a unique tuple is constantly hit. As a side comment, whereas trees perform better under heavy stress scenario, as they balance the depth of the structure in case of random or real traffic, in our implementation that requires two memory access their performance is lower in case of deterministic traffic.

Clearly, performance of all possible real traffic sequences fall in between the two ideal extremes presented in Tab. 1. As part of our future work, we plan to investigate the relationship of flow-matching performance with the entropy of the tuple sequence (e.g., a simple way to interpolate between two extremes is to model the probability of individual IP addresses with a Zipf distribution, and tune the skew α). We have tested with multiple traces and artificial sequences. Ideally, we would like to carry out a worst-case analysis with adversarial traffic, though this is unknown and hard to generate in the case of general hash functions. For future work, we aim at injecting DoS or DDoS attacks (e.g., portscan, netscan, etc.) into real traces.

5   Related Work

Monitoring at the flow level requires matching each packet to the correct flow bin. In software-based solutions such as Bro [25], Snort [29], Tstat [30], CoralReef [5] or YAF [20] this is usually accomplished by using hash-based structures over the flow 5-tuple. In [23] the authors point out that most time-consuming operations in systems such as Bro and Snort, are related to tracking the connections – which precisely motivates this work.

Table 2. Maximum Mfps, Mpps and Gbps processing rates of related work

Category	Ref.	Rates			Comments
		Mfps	Mpps	Gbps	
Flow management	[7]	-	6	10	Endace DAG cards
	[8]	-	17	-	16 cores, 16x1Gbps cards
	[15]	1	10	10	6 cores
	[31]	2.8	14.2	10	2 cores

However, to the best of our knowledge, the performance of flow matching code in complex monitoring and intrusion detection systems is rarely evaluated *in a systematic fashion*. In particular, only limited works report on the performance of the data structure and of the hashing functions being used when implementing such operations [24]. Our work indeed starts from similar viewpoint of [24], that however limitedly focus on the study of hash functions, but extends it to consider a more comprehensive set of design choices (e.g., list vs trees, structure size, etc.). Basically, different systems implement their own strategies and we are not aware of work that investigates the impact of such choices in the design of a flow management module. For instance, [20] describes a flow management module in detail, explaining how to optimize flow management using slab allocator [12] for fast recycling of expired flow records, but benchmarks of the system performance are not publicly available. Otherwise, performance analysis for flow matching modules has been done either monitoring real ISP deployments [17] or over offline traces [23, 30, 33]. Comparing the performance of flow management modules of heterogeneous systems (e.g., Bro, Snort, Tstat and YAF) is hard since the *full set* of operations performed beyond flow-management are different, and so are the traces used as input to the evaluation. As such, extrapolating such data from overall measurements [17, 20, 23, 30, 33] can be misleading: to prevent this risk, we rely on publicly available dataset and software.

Explicit performance for systems using dedicated hardware is reported instead in [7, 8, 15, 26, 32], that we summarize in Tab. 2. In [7], using a dual Xeon box hosting a dedicate Endace DAG card, authors match flows at a rate up to 6 Mpps. In [26] an Intel IXP2850 Network Processor is shown matching 10 million concurrent flows at 10 Gbps at full packet rate. Switching to off-the-shelf setup, an application note from Intel [8] reports flow matching of trains of 64 bytes packets at 17 Mpps out of 24 Mpps received over 16× 1 Gbps interfaces, where each NIC is tied to a different core of an Intel multi-core CPU system (unfortunately the study does not report the number of concurrent flows). A similar architecture [15] matches up to 11Mpps for 1 million concurrent flows at 10Gbps using "FastFlow" algorithms spawned over 6 cores. Instead, the software-based system we proposed in [31], handles aggregate flow rates up to 2.8Mfps using just two cores. Knowledge gathered in this work can hopefully extend further these performance through a fine tuning of the flow management module.

6   Conclusion and Perspective

This work ventures in the flow management component common to all traffic monitors and analyzers. We take a systematic approach, and study the impact of hash functions, data structure design and sizes in the flow management performance. Employing a trace-driven emulation approach, that allows to jointly gather realistic performance while studying a large design space at the same time, we unveil several tradeoffs in this exploration.

We can summarize our main lessons as:

- *Balanced trees are inherently more robust* to misconfiguration with respect to lists, limiting performance losses.
- *Balanced trees are inherently more complex to manage*, to the point that frequent memory operations may erode the advantage over simples structures such as lists, where infrequent collisions in case of properly configured structure sizes, translate into fewer memory operations.
- *Hash functions play a minor role*, at least when structures are properly sized, with computational complexity eroding the advantage of hashes with better entropy properties.

Clearly, this work is by no means complete: expansions can include a larger spectrum of *hash functions* (e.g., CRC32, One-at-a-Time, FNV [9], Hsieh [6] among others, especially aiming at lower computational complexity) or *data structures* (e.g., double hash, cuckoo hashing [34], denser hashes as in DPDK [10]).

Additionally, low-level system aspects such as memory management, including translation lookaside buffer, memory fragmentation and alignment, and NUMA allocation (the latter considered by us in [31]), likely play an important role and deserve attention.

A second direction is to replicate this study over a *wider dataset* including traces from different network segments, in an attempt to find consistently good setting that can be recommended for different environments. A useful extension of this work would be to correlate flow-management performance (e.g., matching rate, chain length, tree depth, etc.) with *key characteristics* of the network traffic (e.g., distributions of address space, spatio-temporal correlation of arrivals, etc.) to also offer a methodology for a semi-automatic fine-grained tuning of the above data structures.

Security is another interesting topic that, due to space constraints, was left out of the scope of this paper (see [16] and references therein). For future work, we aim at injecting DoS or DDoS attacks (e.g., portscan, netscan, etc.) into real traces, and to investigate adversarial scenarios (leading to hash table collision). Such adversarial *synthetic patterns* could be super-imposed over real traces: as due their distributed nature, with possibly spoofed addresses, attacks could be used to stress-test the flow management architectures. Additionally, this would also allow to tune the level of randomness between real vs random traffic, by specifying the intensity of the synthetic pattern with respect to the normal traffic.

Acknowledgement. This work has been carried out at LINCS http://www.lincs.fr. The research leading to these results has received funding from the European Union under the FP7 Grant Agreement n. 318627 (Integrated Project "mPlane").

References

1. http://www.cisco.com/en/US/solutions/collateral/ns341/ns525/ns537/ns705/ns827/white_paper_c11-481360.pdf
2. http://www.ing.unibs.it/ntw/tools/fmsim
3. http://www.caida.org/data/passive/trace_stats/
4. http://burtleburtle.net/bob/
5. http://www.caida.org/tools/measurement/coralreef/dists/coral-3.9.1.tar.gz
6. http://www.azillionmonkeys.com/qed/hash.html
7. http://www.terena.org/activities/ngn-ws/ws2/deri-10g.pdf
8. http://download.intel.com/design/intarch/papers/322516.pdf
9. http://www.isthe.com/chongo/tech/comp/fnv/
10. http://www.dpdk.org
11. Bonelli, N., Di Pietro, A., Giordano, S., Procissi, G.: On multi–gigabit packet capturing with multi–core commodity hardware. In: Taft, N., Ricciato, F. (eds.) PAM 2012. LNCS, vol. 7192, pp. 64–73. Springer, Heidelberg (2012)
12. Bonwick, J.: The slab allocator: An object-caching kernel memory allocator. In: USENIX Summer Technical Conference (1994)
13. Cardigliano, A., Deri, L., Gasparakis, J., Fusco, F.: vPF_RING: Towards wire-speed network monitoring using virtual machines. In: ACM IMC (2011)
14. Crotti, M., Dusi, M., Gringoli, F., Salgarelli, L.: Traffic classification through simple statistical fingerprinting. ACM SIGCOMM Comput. Commun. Rev. 37(1), 5–16 (2007)
15. Danelutto, M., Deri, L., De Sensi, D.: Network monitoring on multicores with algorithmic skeletons. In: International Conference on Parallel Computing, PARCO (2011)
16. Eckhoff, D., Limmer, T., Dressler, F.: Hash tables for efficient flow monitoring: vulnerabilities and countermeasures. In: IEEE LCN (2009)
17. Finamore, A., Mellia, M., Meo, M., Munafo, M., Rossi, D.: Experiences of Internet traffic monitoring with Tstat. IEEE Network 25(3), 8–14 (2011)
18. Fusco, F., Deri, L.: High speed network traffic analysis with commodity multi-core systems. In: ACM IMC (2010)
19. Han, S., Jang, K., Park, K., Moon, S.: PacketShader: a GPU-accelerated software router. In: ACM SIGCOMM (2010)
20. Inacio, C., Trammell, B.: YAF: yet another flowmeter. In: International Conference on Large Installation System Administration, LISA (2010)
21. Knuth, D.E.: The art of computer programming (1968)
22. Lim, Y., Kim, H., Jeong, J., Kim, C., Kwon, T., Choi, Y.: Internet traffic classification demystified: on the sources of the discriminative power. In: ACM CoNEXT (2010)
23. Lin, P.-C., Lee, J.-H.: Re-examining the performance bottleneck in a nids with detailed profiling. Journal of Network and Computer Applications 36(2), 768–780 (2013)
24. Molina, M., Niccolini, S., Duffield, N.: A comparative experimental study of hash functions applied to packet sampling. In: International Teletraffic Congress, ITC (2005)
25. Paxson, V.: Bro: a system for detecting network intruders in real-time. Computer Networks 31(23-24), 2435–2463 (1999)
26. Qi, Y., Xu, B., He, F., Yang, B., Yu, J., Li, J.: Towards high-performance flow-level packet processing on multi-core network processors. In: ACM/IEEE ANCS (2007)
27. Rizzo, L.: Netmap: a novel framework for fast packet I/O. In: USENIX Annual Technical Conference (2012)
28. Rizzo, L., Carbone, M., Catalli, G.: Transparent acceleration of software packet forwarding using netmap. In: IEEE INFOCOM (2012)

29. Roesch, M.: Snort - lightweight intrusion detection for networks. In: USENIX Conference on System Administration (1999)
30. Rossi, D., Mellia, M.: Real-time TCP/IP analysis with common hardware. In: IEEE ICC (2006)
31. Santiago del Río, P.M., Rossi, D., Gringoli, F., Nava, L., Salgarelli, L., Aracil, J.: Wire-speed statistical classification of network traffic on commodity hardware. In: ACM IMC (2012)
32. Srinivasan, D., Feng, W.: Performance analysis of multi-dimensional packet classification on programmable network processors. Computer Communications 28(15), 1752–1760 (2005)
33. Wang, D., Xue, Y., Dong, Y.: Memory-efficient hypercube flow table for packet processing on multi-cores. In: IEEE GLOBECOM (2011)
34. Zhou, D., Fan, B., Lim, H., Kaminsky, M., Andersen, D.G.: Scalable, high performance ethernet forwarding with cuckooswitch. In: ACM CoNEXT (2013)

Inline Data Integrity Signals
for Passive Measurement

Brian Trammell[1], David Gugelmann[1], and Nevil Brownlee[2]

[1] Communication Systems Group, ETH Zurich, Switzerland
[2] Dept. of Computer Science, University of Auckland, New Zealand

Abstract. In passive network measurement, the quality of an observed traffic stream is obviously crucial to the quality of the results. Some sources of error (e.g., packet loss at a capture device) are well understood, others less so. In this work, we describe the inline data integrity measurement provided by the QoF TCP-aware flow meter. By instrumenting the data structures QoF uses for detecting lost and retransmitted TCP segments, we can provide an in-band, per-flow estimate of observation loss: segments which were received by the recipient but not observed by the flow meter. We evaluate this mechanism against controlled, induced error, and apply it to two data sets used in previous work.

1 Introduction and Related Work

Network measurement is the practice of examining traffic data in order to deduce or derive information about the properties of the measured network. This traffic can either be generated for the purposes of measurement (in active measurement), or can be generated by the network's users (in passive measurement). In all cases, the measurement infrastructure itself injects some error or bias into the measurement, such that interpretation of the results must take care to account for this error. This fact is too often ignored in the network measurement literature.

Measurement studies can use control traffic with known parameters to provide ground truth, whether part of the protocol for active measurements, or injected alongside the measured traffic for passive measurements. In all cases, the data produced are a function of the actual traffic measured, the mismatch between the assumed and actual behavior of the network, and inaccuracies injected by design or implementation flaws in measurement tools.

Even the simplest of active measurement approaches, the venerable `ping` utility, is not immune from this conflict between the ideal and the real. For example, Pelsser et al [1] recently found that two-way delay measured across a link by `ping` can have significant dependencies on the flow identifier, an artifact of in-path load balancing.

It is harder to control for these errors in passive measurement than active measurement, and the mismatch between real and assumed behavior of the measurement tools plays a greater role. For example, Hofstede et al [2] characterized

A. Dainotti, A. Mahanti, and S. Uhlig (Eds.): TMA 2014, LNCS 8406, pp. 15–25, 2014.

inaccuracy in timing and TCP flags in NetFlow data in three commercial flow meters. Cunha et al [3] detailed timing errors in publicly available Abilene and GEANT flow traces injected by Juniper's J-Flow. An author of the present work [4] even found timing error inherent in the design of Cisco's Netflow Version 9 protocol. Error injected by passive measurement design, implementation, and deployment issues was treated systematically by Kögel [5], who advocated exporter profiling to correct for these errors post-measurement.

In this paper, we consider the QoF (pronounced "quaff") TCP-aware flow meter, which leverages the flexibility of the IPFIX [6] protocol to export per-flow statistics relevant to TCP performance. QoF was developed to allow per-flow observation of TCP flows, for operational troubleshooting as well as for research purposes. As such, it requires precise timing for the estimation of TCP round-trip time (RTT) as well as very low or no *observation loss* – packets which were delivered, but not observed. Because QoF is a purely passive flow meter, a self-validation approach using injected traffic is not an option. Therefore, we sought to observe signals present in the data in order to increase our confidence about the suitability of the data for the measurement techniques employed by QoF.

We instrumented QoF's data structures for signaling detected gaps in the input data in order to report on observation loss. The literature on the effects of packet sampling treats the problem of known random observation loss on the fidelity of flow data [7,8]; a key contribution of the present work, in essence, is the export of information about the *unknown*, not necessarily random sampling attributable to a measurement infrastructure, and export of this information along with measured data, so that it can be used in subsequent analysis. While this information is often available in the logs of flow meters and analysis tools, QoF's approach of providing information on loss *in-band* greatly increases its usefulness.

In this paper, we briefly introduce QoF and the techniques it uses for passive TCP performance measurement, as background for understanding the data integrity checking approach it uses, in section 2. We then detail the methodology for observation loss and timestamp frequency variance measurement in section 3, and apply it to several data sets and network observation points in 5. We note that the tool is particularly applicable to the verification of packet and flow data quality in research applications.

2   Background

QoF is a fork of the CERT Network Situational Awareness Group's YAF (Yet Another Flowmeter) [9]. Our fork of the code removes all payload inspection and export facilities from YAF to increase performance and reduce end-user privacy risk, and replaces the packet capture code with WAND's libtrace [10] to add flexibility and accelerate capture with general-purpose network interfaces. The overall goal is to produce a flow meter operating on unsampled packet header observations which is useful for both performance research and operational purposes. Performance is an explicit design goal, so we avoid techniques

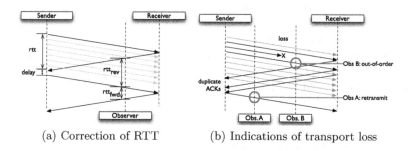

(a) Correction of RTT   (b) Indications of transport loss

Fig. 1. Effects of observer placement on TCP observations

which marginally improve accuracy at the cost of significant analysis or state requirements at the metering process.

Additional functionality in QoF includes passive RTT and transport loss event estimation. As round-trip time (RTT) is a basic parameter of all TCP connections, passive measurement of RTT is a fairly well studied area. QoF uses an approach based on previous work in the area [11,12].

As in figure 1(a), RTT is estimated by adding the interval between seeing a sequence number and the corresponding ACK RTT_{fwd} to the interval between seeing the sequence number in the reverse direction and the corresponding ACK RTT_{rev}. Since many flows are mainly unidirectional, QoF also uses intervals between a TCP timestamp value on a pure ACK and its corresponding echo as well. In contrast to the method described in [13], timestamp echoes are considered only if they would decrease or keep equal the estimate for the component on which they were measured; this simple heuristic serves to minimize *delay*, especially that due to an application not having data to send.

QoF estimates transport loss – packets that did not arrive at the receiver – by observing the sequence of TCP sequence numbers. QoF tracks the initial sequence number as well as the next-expected sequence number in each direction of a flow. Since gaps in the sequence number space should be relatively rare – occurring transiently and refilled within an RTT in most cases – the module tracks gaps in a *gap stack* per flow direction.

Each unseen range in sequence number space is kept in descending order of sequence number. When a segment is observed that begins beyond the next expected sequence number, an out-of-order segment is signaled and the resulting gap is pushed onto the gap stack. Conversely, when a segment is observed that does not advance the sequence number, it is compared with the gaps in the gap stack, most recent gap first. If covering a gap, the gap is filled; otherwise, a retransmission is signaled.

If a loss occurs in the path after the observation point (Observer A in figure 1(b)), the observer will see the retransmitted segment(s) up to one RTT after the loss occurred. If the loss occurs in the path before the observation point (Observer B), the observer will see a gap in sequence number space immediately after the loss, but not observe a retransmission; the size of the gap in the sequence number space is an indication of how many segments were lost. QoF handles spurious retransmissions in part by grouping transport loss indications into RTT-sized windows.

These two features complement each other, and assume the observation of every packet in each flow in order to work properly: transport loss requires the whole sequence of sequence numbers, and RTT estimates on missing ACKs and timestamp echos would be erroneously long. We therefore sought indications in the measured data that this assumption holds.

3 Observation Loss Methodology

In contrast to transport loss, *observation loss* occurs when a packet arrives at the receiver but is not seen by the observation point. We use the gap stack to measure observation loss as well as transport loss. Gaps which are not filled before they are pushed off the stack by newer gaps, or that are still in the gap stack when a flow completes, represent portions of the sequence number space that we presume the TCP receiver saw, since progress through sequence number space continued, but which were not observed by QoF. QoF exports information about observation loss for each direction of each TCP flow.

Packet capture devices and libraries often make available information about how many packets were dropped – partially observed or inferred but not captured – on a per-interface basis. However, this is not the only type of observation loss. For example, packet capture based on packet replication at a switch will fail to observe packets the switch fails to forward down the span port; our method will count this as observation loss as well.

Though this measurement is admittedly rather obvious, the innovation of counting observation loss on a per-flow basis as opposed to a per-interface basis also allows certain analyses to proceed even in the face of unobserved packets, and to investigate any dependencies on packet properties in observation loss. Though we can only caluclate observation loss for TCP flows, we assume that most observation loss processes are transport protocol independent, and can therefore extrapolate observation loss at a given time on a given path for coincident non-TCP traffic.

We note that observation loss measurement using a gap stack is subject to overcounting in three specific conditions. First, the gap stack has a fixed size per flow, so particularly "frothy" flows – those with many reorderings – may have observation loss overcounted, if a gap falls off the end of the stack before it would have been filled. QoF's compiled-in default gapstack size is 8, chosen empirically through analysis a set of test traces. Overcounting due to froth can be reduced by increasing this, at the expense of memory efficiency.

Second, if a gap would be filled after the flow is expired by idle timeout or the observation of a FIN or RST segment, that gap will be counted as observation loss as well. We consider the performance of this structure to be worth the potential overcounting; future work involves additional tweaks to the algorithm to minimize overcounting while maintaining performance. We explore this further in section 5.2.

Additionally, QoF's decoder drops any packet it cannot succeessfully decode, and is paranoid about what it accepts, a legacy of its heritage as a security monitoring tool. This can lead to observation loss caused by QoF itself. QoF also uses a fixed capture length per packet, allowing it to disregard octets it will never use, thereby improving its performance. However, packets where the layer 2, IP, and TCP headers together are longer than the compile-time default of 96 octets, or read from capture files with a shorter snaplen, will lead to observation loss due to such decode failures. This is possible especially in cases of excessive IPv6 encapsulation and/or extension headers. As with the gapstack size, observation loss on long packets can be reduced by increasing the compile-time constant, at the expense of I/O performance.

4   Evaluation

To evaluate the utility of per-flow loss counting to detect impaired measurement, we added detuning functionality to QoF to model packet loss and packet delay in the measurement path[1]. Loss and delay due to residence in a bottleneck queue are modeled using a leaky bucket with a specified size and drain rate. Additionally, we model non-queue-related loss with a test of a specified loss probability against a linearly smoothed uniform random die, and non-queue-related delay using a linearly smoothed uniform delay generator. Since QoF is built under the assumption that packet timestamps are monotonic strictly not decreasing, all delay imparted by the detune module is clamped to a minimum value in order to avoid reordering packets.

We then tested against a publicly available trace from the WIDE MAWI Working Group Traffic Archive[2], taken from a 150Mb/s transpacific link over a three hour period on 30 March 2012, containing 386.2 million packets. The peak flow concurrency [14] is 307.6 thousand concurrent flows (with 63s idle and 300s active timeouts). Reflecting the fact that the trace is taken from a backbone, 72.6% of observed flows are one-way due to asymmetric routing[3]. We assume, but cannot confirm, that actual observation loss in the MAWI traces is negligble.

This evaluation shows, unsurprisingly, that there is a strong relationship between the proportion of flows with reported observation loss and the induced packet drop rate. The function of this relationship is determined by the type of loss induced. For leaky bucket loss with induced packet loss rate varying from 0.00289 to 0.138 and a queue length of 100ms, this function is linear ($slope = 0.136$, $intercept = 3.44 \times 10^{-4}$, $corr = 0.996$). This technique is sensitive even to very low packet loss rates; dropping only 246 packets from 386.2 million led to 70 flows being detected with observation loss.

---

[1] As these features are only useful in the context of this evaluation, they are only enabled in QoF when the `--enable-detune` flag is given to QoF's build configuration script.

[2] http://mawi.wide.ad.jp/mawi/

[3] While QoF is a biflow meter, integrity checking does not require observation of both sides of the flow to work properly, so this evaluation treats each uniflow in a biflow separately.

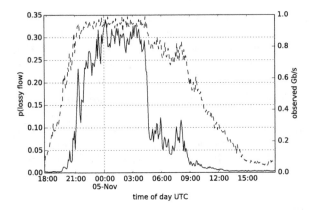

Fig. 2. Daily seasonality of flow loss (solid line) and observed data rate (dashed) on a typical day at Auckland

The dominance of short flows in Internet traffic [14] means that packet loss will lead to unobserved flows, as well. In this evaluation, for each flow with measured observation loss, about four flows went unobserved.

The queue modeled by leaky bucket loss also induces error in packet timings, which changes QoF's estimation of round trip times: the median of the minimum estimated RTT of flows in the MAWI data set is 101ms; this shifts to 110ms using an induced drop rate of 0.302 (i.e., on the order of the loss seen in the Auckland data set treated in section 5.1 below). Since loss due to queueing or buffering (e.g., at a span port or on a capture device) is the dominant type of loss we assume, we note that this indicates that observing loss in a data set also indicates that the timings should not be trusted in further analysis.

5   Findings

Here we apply QoF's per-flow loss reporting features to ongoing data collection efforts on various research networks which have been used in recent publications. The goal here is to verify that the data source used in these works has appropriate observation loss characteristics for the analysis done.

5.1   Auckland and Iatmon

We first applied this methodology to an observation point at the University of Auckland, implemented using a span port on inbound and outbound traffic at the campus border. During the daytime traffic peak at about 11:00 local time (12:00 UTC), we routinely found between 25% and 35% of observed flows reporting observation loss. On further investigation, we found that a span port originally configured to forward approximately 100 Mb/s of traffic in each direction over a Gigabit Ethernet interface was now being offered approximately 700 Mb/s of

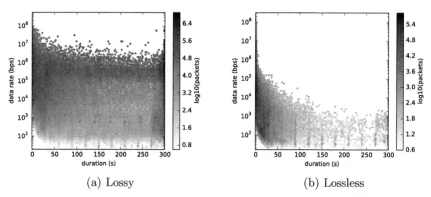

(a) Lossy   (b) Lossless

Fig. 3. Packets by mean data rate and duration of flow during a peak hour at Auckland: note that observation loss affects long-duration, high-rate flows disproportionately

traffic in each direction at peak. Since 1400 Mb/s of traffic will not fit on a 1000 Mb/s link, the span port did not forward about a third of the packets to the observation point.

For the last two years the University's network operations group has been working towards upgrading its Internet-facing infrastructure, including the monitoring and measurement infrastructure. Unfortunately, this requires forklift upgrades to firewalls and boundary routers, and progress is slow. Taking a more positive view, we regard this as a chance to investigate the effects of high observation loss on traffic analysis.

In figure 2, we show the evolution of the dropped flow rate over a typical day (Tuesday, November 5, 2013). Flows experiencing observation loss during the peak hour have a significantly different shape from those which escape the span port lossless. Compare the subfigures in figure 3: while simply dropping the lossy flows in an analysis would lead to retaining about two-thirds of the flows, most of the long-duration, high-rate traffic, and therefore most of the packets, would be missing.

In [15], we monitored one-way traffic using `iatmon`, which measures interarrival time for packets from unsolicited trafic, and classifies such flows into ten groups based on their IAT distributions. That paper used data from the UCSD Network Telescope, i.e. header-trace data for only one-way flows.

However, we also run `iatmon` at Auckland using the same observation point as for our QoF work. At Auckland, `iatmon` filters out the one-way flows from the total traffic – one-way traffic accounts for about 3.5% of the observed packets but about 35% of the observed flows. `iatmon`'s 'flow group' classification is fairly coarse-grained, relying only on the overall features of the IAT distributions. so it should not be affected by our high observation loss rate. However, one-way flows with only a few packets – say 10 or fewer – may not be observed, thereby distorting the distribution of flows between groups.

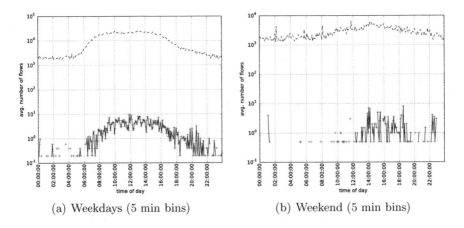

(a) Weekdays (5 min bins)   (b) Weekend (5 min bins)

Fig. 4. Average daily seasonality of flows with detected observation loss (solid line) and total number of flows (dashed line) as observed by QoF

5.2 Horizon Extender

We then applied this methodology to HTTP traces captured at the border router of an university network. Similar to the Auckland setup, packets from the 10 Gb/s inbound and 10 Gb/s outbound link of the main router are forwarded via a single 10 Gb/s span port to the capturing device. A Myricom 10G network adapter in combination with tcpdump is used for traffic capturing. Packets are filtered before being written to disk. The network data analyzed in the following cover IPv4 TCP port 80 traffic of clients in a selected subnetwork of the university that have been recorded during 5 work days and one weekend in late 2012. The total IP-level raw size of the analyzed traces is 1.2 TB of incoming and 43 GB of outgoing traffic, which correspond to 15M TCP streams accounting for 1.2 TB[4] of incoming and 23 GB of outgoing TCP payload data.

The Myricom driver on the capturing device reported no packet loss due to ring-buffer overflow, but since the 10 Gb/s up- and downstream traffic are mirrored over a single 10 Gb/s span port, packets could have been lost at the router. Here we use QoF to show that this was most likely not the case, and compare results to logs from the Bro IDS [16].

The recorded traces have been used to evaluate *Horizon Extender* [17], an approach to archive HTTP data for data leakage investigations. Because it is impossible to fully reconstruct HTTP request and response streams from TCP streams with packet loss, it was important for the evaluation that packet traces of high quality were available, that is, with as little observation loss as possible.

Figure 4 shows the average number of flows and flows with detected observation loss as observed by QoF. The rate of such flows is on the order of 2×10^{-4} overall.

---

[4] Since HTTP is highly asymmetric, incoming traffic is dominated by large flows, so IP layer overhead is negligible.

Analyzing the number of distinct clients and servers for which observation loss was observed in more detail, we found on a single weekday that while we observe on average 5 ± 6 lossy flows per 15 minute time bin, only 3 ± 3 clients and 4 ± 4 servers are affected per time bin. In other words, certain paths between clients and servers are more likely to be affected by observation loss.

We then compared this observation loss rate to the byte loss rate reported by the TCP stream reconstruction engine in Bro, which analyzes complete packet payloads, and assembles them into full streams, as opposed to analyzing just headers as QoF does. We note that Bro reported missing bytes in on the order 10^{-5} of the flows it counted[5]. Upon further investigation, we found potential faults in Bro that would lead to *undercounting* of observation loss, and reported these to the Bro mailing list; a quantification of this undercounting and correction thereof are subjects for future work.

While QoF in this configuration required 29 s to analyze 31 GB of traffic[6], Bro required 730 s in its default configuration and 92 s in bare mode with the connection analyzer only; i.e., QoF is 25 times faster than Bro's default configuration, and still more than three times faster than bare mode, respectively.

In summary, as even a lossy flow rate on the order to 2 per 10000 is acceptable for our analysis of Horizon Extender, we consider our analysis validated by this check. Further, the lack of any evidence of large groups of lossy flows, as with the leaky bucket used in the evaluation, indicates that the span port from which we captured traffic was never significantly overloaded.

6 Conclusions

In this work, we have shown the value of inline data integrity reporting for passive measurement, in the context of the QoF TCP-aware flow metering tool. Presently ongoing work includes the application of QoF to other data sets, and further investigation of other signals available in passively observed TCP traffic, e.g. timestamp frequencies from many TCP stacks, which provide an external timing reference for isolating timing jitter at observation points.

Future developments in QoF can be followed in source form: QoF is available under the GNU General Public License, and is under active development. The latest version is always available from `http://github.com/britram/qof`[7].

Acknowledgments. This work was materially supported by the European Commission though the Seventh Framework Grant Agreement mPlane (FP7-318627); no endorsement of the work by the Commission is implied. Many thanks

---

[5] For comparisons to Bro, we set QoF's active timeout to 1 hour (as opposed to the default, 5 minutes) to reduce timeout-based overcounting, based on our model of potential loss overcounting in QoF (see section 3).

[6] To provide the required data rate for this experiment, the packets have been read from a pcap file that was stored on a ramfs.

[7] The code used in writing this paper is in the `albula` branch, while the `master` branch will always contain a stable version of the most recent feature set.

to Shane Alcock, Bernhard Ager, Jeff Boote, Mirja Kühlewind, and Jinyao Yan for the fruitful discussions during QoF's development; to Emily Sarneso, Chris Inacio, and the CERT Network Situational Awareness Group for further developing YAF, on which QoF is based; and to ITS at the University of Auckland for one of the data sets used in the development of this study.

References

1. Pelsser, C., Cittadini, L., Vissicchio, S., Bush, R.: From Paris to Tokyo: On the suitability of ping to Measure Latency. In: Internet Measurement Conference 2013, Barcelona, Spain, pp. 125–131 (October 2013)
2. Hofstede, R., Drago, I., Sperotto, A., Sadre, R., Pras, A.: Measurement Artifacts in NetFlow Data. In: Roughan, M., Chang, R. (eds.) PAM 2013. LNCS, vol. 7799, pp. 1–10. Springer, Heidelberg (2013)
3. Cunha, Í., Silveira, F., Oliveira, R., Teixeira, R., Diot, C.: Uncovering artifacts of flow measurement tools. In: Moon, S.B., Teixeira, R., Uhlig, S. (eds.) PAM 2009. LNCS, vol. 5448, pp. 187–196. Springer, Heidelberg (2009)
4. Trammell, B., Tellenbach, B., Schatzmann, D., Burkhart, M.: Peeling Away Timing Error in NetFlow Data. In: Spring, N., Riley, G.F. (eds.) PAM 2011. LNCS, vol. 6579, pp. 194–203. Springer, Heidelberg (2011)
5. Kögel, J.: One-way delay measurement based on flow data: Quantification and compensation of errors by exporter profiling. In: ICOIN, pp. 25–30 (2011)
6. Claise, B., Trammell, B., Aitken, P.: Specification of the IP Flow Information Export (IPFIX) Protocol for the Exchange of IP Flow Information. RFC 7011 (Internet Standard) (September 2013)
7. Brauckhoff, D., Tellenbach, B., Wagner, A., May, M., Lakhina, A.: Impact of Packet Sampling on Anomaly Detection Metrics. In: Internet Measurement Conference 2006, Rio de Janerio, Brazil (October 2006)
8. Zseby, T., Hirsch, T., Claise, B.: Packet Sampling for Flow Accounting: Challenges and Limitations. In: Claypool, M., Uhlig, S. (eds.) PAM 2008. LNCS, vol. 4979, pp. 61–71. Springer, Heidelberg (2008)
9. Inacio, C., Trammell, B.: Yaf: Yet another flowmeter. In: Proceedings of the 24th Large Installation System Administration Conference (LISA 2010), San Jose, California, USA, pp. 107–118. USENIX Association (November 2010)
10. Alcock, S., Lorier, P., Nelson, R.: Libtrace: a packet capture and analysis library. SIGCOMM Comput. Commun. Rev. 42(2), 42–48 (2012)
11. Veal, B., Li, K., Lowenthal, D.: New methods for passive estimation of TCP round-trip times. In: Dovrolis, C. (ed.) PAM 2005. LNCS, vol. 3431, pp. 121–134. Springer, Heidelberg (2005)
12. Mellia, M., Meo, M., Muscariello, L., Rossi, D.: Passive analysis of tcp anomalies. Computer Networks 52(14), 2663–2676 (2008)
13. Strowes, S.D.: Passively measuring tcp round-trip times. Communications of the ACM 56(10) (October 2013)
14. Trammell, B., Schatzmann, D.: On Flow Concurrency in the Internet and its Implications for Capacity Sharing. In: Proceedings of the Second ACM CoNext Capacity Sharing Workshop (CSWS), Nice, France (December 2012)

15. Brownlee, N.: One-Way Traffic Monitoring with iatmon. In: Taft, N., Ricciato, F. (eds.) PAM 2012. LNCS, vol. 7192, pp. 179–188. Springer, Heidelberg (2012)
16. Paxson, V.: Bro: a system for detecting network intruders in real-time. Computer Networks 31, 2435–2463 (1999)
17. Gugelmann, D., Schatzmann, D., Lenders, V.: Horizon Extender: Long-term Preservation of Data Leakage Evidence in Web Traffic. In: Proceedings of the 8th ACM SIGSAC Symposium on Information, Computer and Communications Security, Hangzhou, China, pp. 499–504 (2013)

Scalable High Resolution Traffic Heatmaps: Coherent Queue Visualization for Datacenters

Andreea Anghel, Robert Birke, and Mitch Gusat

IBM Research, Zurich, Switzerland
{aan,bir,mig}@zurich.ibm.com

Abstract. We propose a new high resolution – temporal and spatial – 10 Gbps Ethernet monitoring technique based on time-coherent congestion 'heatmaps', revealing (all) the queue occupancies at μs granularity. Notably, queues are sampled with a slightly modified version of the new commodity Ethernet hardware congestion management protocol, i.e., IEEE 802 Quantized Congestion Notification. Our technique is evaluated through high-accuracy Layer-2 simulations of a 10 Gbps datacenter Ethernet fabric. Early results reveal that our proposal enables the detection of ephemeral – yet consequential – events and transients essential for datacenter workload characterization: e.g., TCP Incast, Head-of-Line blocking and congestion trees, which may trigger within 10s of μs and were not directly detectable until now.

Keywords: Network monitoring, L2 sampling, Traffic analysis, QCN.

1 Introduction

The proliferation of Big Data applications – such as Hadoop, MapReduce – together with 10-100 Gbps datacenter networks (DCNs) – such as Converged Enhanced Ethernet (CEE), with μs latency – raises new challenges. One of them is the need for faster and scalable network monitoring methods. Deep understanding of such workloads and their communication patterns is key to the design of future workload-optimized datacenters. For example, the ability to accurately detect and optimize (via adapted routing) workload-induced congestion at fine granularity has significant potential in terms of reducing system cost and improving the application run-time [1]. Switches today have outdated monitoring software that cannot cope with the sampling frequency and the network scale needed to orchestrate large datacenters. Hence our target is to coherently (i.e., time-space synchronized) and scalably detect, record and replay ephemeral – yet consequential – transients, essential for workload characterization: e.g., TCP Incast [2], Head-of-Line blocking [3], and congestion trees [4], phenomena that may trigger within few 10s of μs and significantly affect the network and workload performance.

To address these issues, a significant improvement is required in the way we design and implement network monitoring. The challenges of 10-100 Gbps load monitoring and visualization for high resolution datacenter network management

A. Dainotti, A. Mahanti, and S. Uhlig (Eds.): TMA 2014, LNCS 8406, pp. 26–37, 2014.
© IFIP International Federation for Information Processing 2014

are three-fold. Space-wise, how to collect, correlate and visualize several 1000s of queues, quasi-simultaneously (correlation may be due to either Hadoop/HPC-like workload phases, or the activation of low-level flow control). Time-wise, we face a resolution challenge, i.e., the "μs wall" – one must detect, record, visualize, and/or react to network events that happen at μs (packet duration) timescales. Finally, the method must conceptually scale to million-node datacenters and Tbps link speeds. Hence the need for commodity hardware queue samplers, possibly reusing existing resources. All while helping the users and operators to better understand their load dynamics and nature.

As an exemplary Big Data workload, the Hadoop Partition/Aggregate pattern consists of multiple congestive episodes within few 100s of μs, known as TCP Incasts. The Aggregate phases actually determine the load, dynamic behavior, stability, and finally the user-perceived performance. However, the Incast phases at and above 10 Gbps are too volatile for the current sFlow [5], NetFlow [6], and SNMP [7] monitoring techniques. Hence the need for a faster and lighter load sensing method able to 'catch' such ephemerally volatile *correlated* transients, scale to large networks, and also drill-in, i.e., zoom into a region of interest of a few 10s-100s queues.

We therefore propose a high-resolution (both) temporal and spatial monitoring technique based on IEEE 802 Quantized Congestion Notification (QCN) [8], Ethernet's new congestion management protocol. Triggering, sampling, aggregating, communicating and visualizing network events are based on the concept of time-coherent *snapshots* of the queue occupancy levels. Coherency is achieved by using a network time difference estimation protocol implemented by the switches – a high accuracy alternative to current clock synchronization protocols such as GPS, NTP [9], and IEEE 1588 [10]. We validate the above via simulations using accurate Layer-2 CEE-compliant 10 Gbps fabric models. As a first, our method detects and captures in real time the TCP Incast-like events in *lossless* fabrics, revealing their inception, evolution and global dynamic behavior at μs scale.

2   Selected Related Work

The area of network monitoring, telemetry and topography is exceedingly rich in literature. However, practically only a few schemes have been widely adopted by hardware and software vendors. Thus, despite much larger and faster DCNs, the current state of the art in hardware network monitoring has remained limited to sampling a few, possibly isolated, links with a granularity in the 0.01s to 1s range: e.g., sFlow, NetFlow and SNMP. These methods we consider insufficient for today's 10/100 Gbps DCNs and large distributed workloads.

More recent proposals, such as [11], suggest new router extensions to perform path sampling using hardware synchronization via IEEE 1588. By instrumenting switches with a hash-based primitive, the authors measure latencies down to 10s of μs and 1 loss in a million. By contrast, our proposal (ab)uses the QCN standard to sample queues (instead of paths) with a theoretical sub-μs sampling.

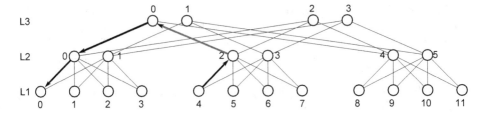

Fig. 1. Folded topology representation of XGFT(3;2,4,3;1,2,2). Links are bidirectional. Node levels start at 0 from bottom to top (L0 to L3). Nodes within a level start at 0 from left to right. For simplicity reasons, only the switch levels (L1, L2, L3) are shown. L0 is populated with 2 (nodes) · 12 (L1-switches) = 24 (nodes). We highlight one path from switch 4 on L1 to switch 0 on L1. The red link represents the upstream queue of port 0 at switch 2 on L2.

Batraneanu et al. [12] propose a tool-set developed to demonstrate aggregate achievable cross-sectional bandwidth for specific traffic profiles, as well as to analyze network hot spot behavior. Queues are being monitored at μs using sFlow and an FPGA implementation. Though the achieved timescale is similar, their solution is fundamentally different in various perspectives: we use the readily available QCN queue samplers, provide a coherent globally synchronized trigger-driven method, developed a record-and-replay tool validated in PFC-enabled 10 Gbps CEE networks, and show that our heatmaps scale with low overhead.

Another related proposal [13] identifies the challenges of datacenter and cloud monitoring and visualization: scale, rapidity, difficulties of detection, localization, and diagnose of performance problems. The proposed tool, i.e., Visual-I, relates directly to our targets. However, while we share goals with Visual-I, our method differs on the use of coherent heatmaps and the novel Layer-2 capabilities of the upcoming CEE-based datacenter networks.

3   Traffic Heatmap Method

We propose a matrix-based traffic visualization scheme as follows. Each packet sent from a source to a destination follows a certain route in the network, as depicted in Fig. 1, and travels through the corresponding set of queues in the forwarding switches, contributing to their respective occupancies. A network congestion/traffic heatmap is an instantaneous time-synchronous 2D snapshot image of the occupancy of all the switch queues in the network. Each heatmap cell represents a single queue providing a fine-grained spatial view of the network.

The occupancy is linearly color-coded on 16 bits using shades of red. The color ranges from white, empty, to dark red, full. Since the heatmaps are time-synchronous, they represent a snapshot of the network queues' status. This allows us to temporally concatenate such sequentially-acquired snapshots into an animated 'movie'. This movie not only provides insights into the network status evolution – congestion levels and locations – but also into the volatile causes and effects of network anomalies such as congestion trees.

The heatmaps are created by a controller which is the central element of the monitoring framework. The forwarding switches sample their queue occupancies – by reusing the commodity QCN hardware mechanism – and send them to the controller (see Subsec. 3.2). The controller then performs two mappings: one in time and one in space. In time, each sample is timestamped using the local clock of the switch it originated from. Since each switch has its own clock, the controller needs to map all the timestamps to a single common timeline (see Subsec. 3.4). The converted timestamps are sorted chronologically. The configuration of the heatmap at any given moment on the timeline is then given by the most recent occupancy value received for every queue previous to that moment. In space, the controller must know the network topology and location of each switch and queue. We assume the existence of a topology discovery protocol that detects and signals topology changes to the controller, for example, through the information gathered by the spanning tree protocol. Each queue has a unique identifier, thus each sample can be mapped to a precise cell using a topology-dependent bijective function. Since we focus on datacenter networks, we only present the mapping for fat trees (Subsec. 3.3). However, our method can be extended to other topologies by changing the mapping bijection.

The final *raw* result is a time-series of complete space-time mappings of all queue occupancy samples of all the switches. The heatmap thus created allows the detection of even ephemeral network anomalies. Once a critical area has been identified – e.g. due to particularly frequent congestion events – it is possible to increase the sampling frequency of those switches/queues to further enhance the detection accuracy. Also, once the culprits are identified, it is possible to take online or offline corrective actions and solve the hotspots or the detected events. An example is given in Sec. 5.1.

3.1   Datacenter Network Topology

Today, fat trees, i.e., multistage k-ary n-fly topologies, are typically the base for large datacenters [14,15]. These topologies can be described by extended generalized fat trees (XGFTs) [16]. An $XGFT(h; m_1, ...m_h; w_1, ...w_h)$ has $h + 1$ node levels divided into leaf and inner nodes. The $\prod_{i=1}^{h} m_i$ leaf nodes reside on level 0 and serve as end nodes/servers. Inner nodes occupy levels 1 to h and serve as switches. Each inner node on level i has m_i child nodes and each non-root node on level j has w_{j+1} parent nodes. Fig. 1 shows an exemplary XGFT(3;2,4,3;1,2,2).

3.2   Load Sensing: Queue Sampling

The queue sampling is performed in a distributed manner: each switch samples its own local queues. Sampling can start either periodically or remotely triggered upon a controller request. In the latter case, the controller sends a request to the switch with the desired sampling duration, rate and start time translated to the switch's own clock. The novelty of our approach consists in extending the

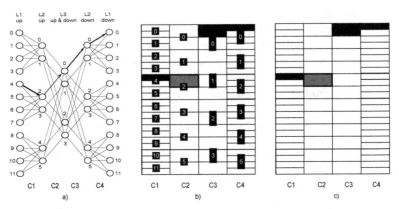

Fig. 2. Spatial mapping example. Intermediate Fig. a) and b) show how the XGFT from Fig. 1 is mapped onto the heatmap in c). a) unfolds and rotates the topology by 90 degrees. Links are unidirectional: traffic flows from left to right. Each level corresponds to the up-/down- stream direction. All figures highlight the same exemplary path from switch 4 on L1 to switch 0 on L1. Similarly, red highlights the send queue(s) of port 0 at switch 2 of level 2 (L2). Each link level in a) corresponds to a column in b) and c). Whereas, each cell in a column represents top-down the output queues ordered by: (1) the switch and (2) the port within that switch. E.g., C3 shows the downstream output queues of the L3 switches: 4 switches · 3 ports · 1 queue = 12 queues. Typical current switches have 1 to 4 hardware queues per port, but for increased clarity of results in paper format we will assume herein a single queue per port – the generalization to several queues is nonetheless trivial.

use of the QCN load sensor to traffic monitoring. QCN is Ethernet's new end-to-end congestion management which, together with its new flow control, i.e., Priority Flow Control (PFC), is being adapted by a growing number of network equipment to ease the network convergence commonly known as CEE.

To detect congestion, QCN uses load sensors monitoring all the queues. Its main objective is to keep the queue occupancy at a target equilibrium Q_{eq}. At each frame arrival, QCN samples with probability π the queue occupancy. For each sampled frame, the load sensor computes a feedback value based on the current and past occupancy. Negative feedbacks are sent back to the frame's source, which reduces its injection rate, thus adjusting it to the available bandwidth.

Extending the use of the QCN load sensor to monitoring has the great benefit of readily available hardware which can sample *all* the queues at fine, i.e. subμs timescales, theoretically even per packet arrival – during limited *zoom-in* sampling intervals.

This improves upon other state of the art monitoring tools both in terms of temporal – 10s of ns – and spatial granularity – each output queue. However two additional steps are needed to enhance the native behavior of QCN's load sampler: (1) to timestamp and locally store the QCN samples; and (2) to make the samples available to the heatmap controller.

To avoid flooding the network with monitoring traffic, we use compressive sampling and filtering based on the feedback values computed by QCN. The

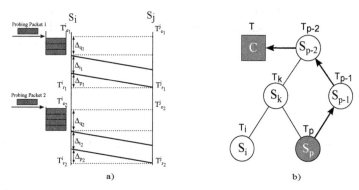

Fig. 3. a) Method to calculate the relative drifts and offsets of two neighboring switches S_i and S_j. b) Method to calculate the absolute drift and offset of a switch S_p to a reference controller system C.

informative samples are mainly related to a congestive event. Hence, all negative feedback samples, signaling a congestion, are sent to the controller. During positive feedback sampling periods, only the first sample is sent back to the controller. During normal network operation, this filter removes most of the samples. To further reduce the monitoring overhead, it is possible to reduce the probability π (see Subsec. 5.3), and compress and aggregate multiple samples into MTU frames. Jumbo frames up to 10-20 KB could be used for high radix switches with thousands of queues (per port and priority). Once the frame is full or upon a timeout – to bound the reporting delay in case of sparse sample reporting – the resulting local snapshot frame is sent to the controller for heatmap assembly.

3.3   XGFT Mapping: Heatmap Bijection

Each heatmap cell represents a specific queue. Fig. 2 shows in steps the heatmap creation of the XGFT in Fig. 1. If level c has S switches, each switch P ports in the upstream/downstream direction, and each port Q queues, then within that level/column, row $r = s \cdot P \cdot Q + p \cdot Q + q$ represents queue q belonging to port p of switch s, where $0 \leqslant s < S$, $0 \leqslant p < P$ and $0 \leqslant q < Q$. Conversely, given a row r within column c, the reverse mapping is: $q = r \bmod Q$, $p = \frac{r}{Q} \bmod P$, $s = \frac{r}{P \cdot Q}$ and the unfolded network level is c. This mapping is valid for homogeneous switches, i.e., same port and queue numbers, which is typical in practice. However, the mapping can be extended to accommodate non-homogeneous configurations. Moreover, although in this paper we only address the mapping of fat tree topologies (which are the most commonly used in datacenters), the mapping can be extended to multi-dimensional topologies by using topological isomorphisms as proposed in [17].

3.4   Coherent Sampling: Clock Difference Estimation Protocol

A coherent network heatmap requires: (1) a snapshot of the queues at the same time instant, i.e., 10s of ns timescale; and (2) a common time reference for the occupancy samples. Since each switch has its own internal clock, this problem is not trivial and goes beyond the scope of this paper. Nevertheless, we shortly introduce a clock estimation method based on the following linear drift model:

$$t_i = \delta_i \cdot t + \omega_i \tag{1}$$

where t is the controller reference time, t_i the time at switch S_i, and δ_i and ω_i the absolute clock drift and offset at switch S_i. We also assume that all δ_i and ω_i are constant and that $\omega_i > 0$. This model entails that given two switches S_i and S_j, we have:

$$t_i = \delta_{ij} \cdot t_j + \omega_{ij} \tag{2}$$

where $\delta_{ij} = \delta_i/\delta_j$ and $\omega_{ij} = \omega_i - \delta_{ij} \cdot \omega_j$ are the relative drift and offset between S_i and S_j.

We rely on an adhoc neighbor-to-neighbor protocol between the switches to minimize estimation errors on the one-way latency due to queuing delays in intermediate hops. Fig. 3a) shows the method to calculate the relative drifts and offsets between two neighboring switches S_i and S_j. S_i sends a probe of size P_s to S_j over a link with speed BW containing the local enqueuing time T_e^i and local queue size Q_s^i. We assume the one-way latency Δ to be the sum of three delays: (i) queuing $\Delta_q = \frac{Q_s}{BW}$, (ii) transmission $\Delta_t = \frac{P_s}{BW}$, and (iii) propagation Δ_p which depends only on the type and cable length, hence assumed to be constant. Using Eq. 1, the arrival time t_r^j at S_j can be expressed as $T_r^j = \delta_{ji} \cdot T + \omega_{ji}$ and $T_r^i = T_e^i + \Delta$. Thus, we have:

$$T_r^j = \delta_{ji} \cdot (T_e^i + \Delta_q + \Delta_t + \Delta_p) + \omega_{ji} \tag{3}$$

containing only three unknowns: δ_{ij}, ω_{ij} and Δ_p. For each probe, the receiving switch adds one equation to an equation system. Solving this system allows to obtain δ_{ji} and ω_{ji}, which are sent to the controller. From all the relative drifts and offsets, the controller then computes the absolute drifts and offsets as shown in Fig. 3b). It computes the absolute δ_i and ω_i for each switch by iteratively applying Eq. 1 on all consecutive switch pairs along the path. The general equation given a switch S_p reachable via the path $S_p \Rightarrow S_{p-1} \Rightarrow \ldots \Rightarrow S_1 \Rightarrow C$ is shown in Eq. 4.

$$t_p = \prod_{i=2}^{p} \delta_{i,i-1} \cdot t + \sum_{i=1}^{p-1} \left(\prod_{j=i}^{p-1} \delta_{j+1,j} \right) \cdot \omega + \omega_{p,p-1} = \delta_p \cdot t + \omega_p \tag{4}$$

This approach allows for a non-intrusive clock compensation without alteration of the internal switch clocks. The temporal correlation among queue samples, as well as among the start/stop sampling commands, is achieved without explicit synchronization of the switch clocks.

4   Network and Simulation Environment

To show the benefits of such monitoring tool, we identify congestion trees in a lossless datacenter network. More in detail, we consider the same XGFT topology as presented in Sec. 3, comprising 24 end nodes and 22 switches interconnected by 10 Gbps CEE-compliant links. CEE aims at providing a reliable Layer-2 in contrast to the conventional Ethernet which drops frames as soon as a buffer reaches its maximum capacity. CEE achieves this by relying on two distinct protocols: PFC and QCN.

Similar to IEEE 802.3x PAUSE, PFC avoids packet losses during congestion by pausing the sender using explicit control frames. However PFC uses the concept of service classes: a paused priority does not affect the others. QCN counteracts

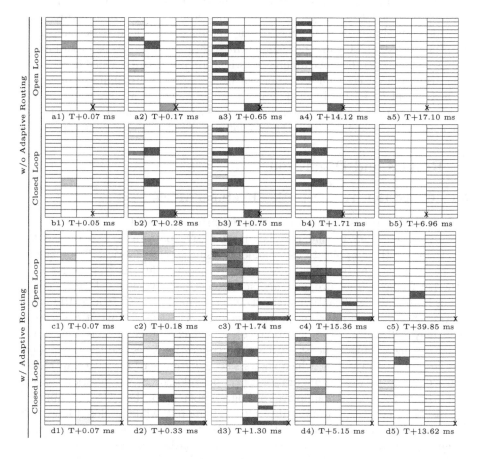

Fig. 4. XGFT(3;2,4,3;1,2,2) under many-to-one traffic (nodes 0-15 send to node 23 at full link speed, i.e. 10 Gbps, for 10 ms starting at T). Each row corresponds to a different network configuration and shows 5 time steps of the congestion evolution. The first 3 steps show the congestion tree onset, while the last 2 steps show the network recovery. The congestion tree root is marked by X.

the congestion entity by limiting the injection rates of the culprit sources. Even if mitigated by QCN, PFC can be affected by Head-of-Line blocking building up into congestion trees in the network: a blocked sender may fill up its buffer and recursively other devices will possibly get paused spreading the congestion backwards. Congestion trees can significantly degrade network performance [4], and hence it is useful to detect them to act quickly on their removal.

The occupancy samples are generated using high-accuracy Layer-2 simulations from an event-driven simulator based on OMNeT++ [18]. The simulator is a two-level architecture network modeling platform. The higher level is the topological or system level where we gain a generic overview of the whole simulated infrastructure as an interconnection of modules. The lower level is that of the internal structure of each network module: e.g., hosts, and switches. We used our own network simulator due to its enhanced support for the CEE standards and detailed models of the Layer-2 switch and adapter micro-architectures. We extended our simulator to include: (1) the modified QCN load sensor additionally timestamping, storing and aggregating the queue samples as described in Subsec. 3.2 and (2) the clock difference estimation protocol described in Sec. 3.4. The drifts and offsets values are derived from empirical distributions obtained by instrumenting an Intel e1000 network driver and by analyzing the speed at which clocks of neighboring systems drift. A JAVA-based application collects the queue occupancy samples from the simulator and generates the heatmaps.

5 Results and Discussion

5.1 Congestion Tree Detection Heatmap Movie

As use case we propose a TCP Incast-like scenario, typical of Partition/Aggregate workloads. This bursty and correlated congestive pattern is also typical for barrier-based HPC applications, commonly using lossless fabrics. The surge in correlated packet arrivals overflows the aggregation buffer. In TCP over legacy Ethernet frames will be dropped, and subsequently recovered via TCP timeouts – thus leading to significantly increased delays. In modern CEE fabrics, PFC prevents such drops and improves performance [19]. However, transient congestion trees may still degrade the performance – under certain conditions: flow sizes, buffer settings, hotspot/incast degree. Such congestion trees and their evolution can be observed in Fig. 4, which shows selected *frames* of the heatmap movie under different network configurations: (a) open/closed QCN congestion control loop; (b) without or with adaptive routing. In open loop, the QCN rate limiters are disabled, i.e., congestion notifications are ignored; while in closed loop, the QCN rate limiters react by adjusting the injection rate. The adaptive routing scheme [20] balances the load over the multiple paths available in fat trees. In contrast to Fig. 2c), each heatmap in Fig. 4 includes one additional column (C5) representing the downstream queues of the L1 switches.

Row (a), i.e., open loop without adaptive routing, shows that the congestion tree fully builds up within 700 μs. Its root, i.e., designated hotspot, is located on the first downstream output queue, the flows convergence point. After 17 ms the congestion tree is drained, no longer affecting the flow delays. Closing the QCN loop (row b) mitigates the congestion as seen both from the lighter shades of red and the $\sim 2.4\times$ shorter draining time (7 ms). As expected, when enabling adaptive routing many more queues share the load - since the traffic is spread across multiple paths (row c and d); now all the 'incast' flows meet only at the destination, relocating the previous tree root. Again closing the QCN loop (row d) reduces the congestion duration, draining faster by a factor $\sim 3\times$. While these results meet the initial expectations, now they are also revealed to external observers without the benefit of apriori knowledge. The events of potential interest are *automatically* detected based on the programmable QCN threshold setpoint, recorded, and visualized for offline analysis.

The fine-grained timescale achievable with our coherent 'snapshooting' method naturally lends itself to movie-like playbacks, with variable temporal resolutions in frames/s. This not only enhances the user experience, but also enables temporal zooming (fast/slow motion, fast forward). Thus we can monitor longer time intervals without loosing track of the – potentially ephemeral – events of interest.

5.2   Time Estimation Accuracy

To test the accuracy of our clock estimation protocol, we use the same network as above, with uniform all-to-all background (i.i.d.) traffic at 60% load. Results show a mean error among all 10 Gbps switches of 380 ns with a standard deviation of 465 ns. The achieved accuracy is comparable to the hardware-aided implementation of IEEE 1588 [21] and 2x-3x better than the software-only IEEE 1588 version [22].

5.3   Monitoring Overhead

The overhead of our QCN-based sampling technique depends on several parameters: average network diameter, injected traffic, average congestion level/severity and its duration. Here we show only the influence of the QCN parameters. In particular we consider the queue sampling probability $\pi \in [1\%, 2\%, 4\%, 10\%]$ and the queue equilibrium setpoint $Q_{eq} \in [2KB, 4KB, 8KB, 16KB]$. We assume a sample size of 8B including a queue identifier (16 bit), queue occupancy (16 bit), queue occupancy variation (16 bit), timestamp offset (16 bit); plus a standard Ethernet-IP-TCP header (54B) extended with a switch identifier 6B and a base timestamp 8B (Timestamp = Base + Offset, for space saving). We compute the sampling overhead as the ratio between the sampling traffic reported to the controller and the total traffic sent by all hosts during the sampling period. The results show that π directly affects the overhead, but even for aggressive sampling probabilities, i.e. 10% (e.g., one in 10 packet arrivals in a 128-port switch fully N-to-1 congested can lead to sub-μs periods at 10 Gbps), the obtained overhead is less than 0.2%. For π of less than 5%, the overhead is below 0.1%. This overhead is approximately constant with respect to Q_{eq}.

5.4 Switch Code Complexity

The additional switch code complexity is low. On the data plane, the switch only needs to locally save and timestamp the occupancy samples already collected by the QCN sampler. On the control plane, the switch needs to perform two sets of operations: (1) aggregate, compress, and send the QCN samples to a centralized controller; (2) collect probes for the clock difference estimation protocol through a heartbeat protocol. The actual derivation of the relative offsets and drifts can be performed either locally or, if too complex for the local switch control processor, offloaded to the controller.

6 Conclusions

We presented a high resolution monitoring method with: (1) μs queue sampling period, (2) based on the newly available IEEE 802 *QCN* hardware load *sensing*; (3) fabric-level *coherence*, i.e., global synchronous trigger-driven method; (4) multi-queue heatmap 'snapshooting' that scales up with low traffic overheads; (5) an intuitive matrix representation of the datacenter system based on a bijective mapping of the common XGFT networks; (6) a record and replay *visualization* tool, validated in lossless link-level flow-controlled 10 Gbps accurate Layer-2 simulations.

As proof of concept, we have designed and implemented a method that displays the time-coherent heatmap snapshots and movies showing the simultaneous occupancy of – some or all – the queues in a simulated network. For the first time now, the detection and visualization – in quasi-real time – of congestion trees and Incast events, correlated across the entire fabric, have been shown to operate in a lossless 10 Gbps commodity Ethernet. Thus, this method enables finer resolution insights into workload-specific traffic patterns and detects persistent and transient anomalies. This fast and efficient monitoring approach can benefit researchers, architects, network administrators, Big Data application developers, etc., to better understand the interaction between complex workloads and the underlying networks in large multitenant datacenters.

References

1. Prisacari, B., et al.: Fast pattern-specific routing for fat tree networks. ACM TACO 10(4), 36:1–36:25 (2013)
2. Zhang, J., et al.: Modeling and understanding TCP incast in data center networks. In: IEEE INFOCOM, pp. 1377–1385 (2011)
3. Jurczyk, M., et al.: Phenomenon of higher order head-of-line blocking in multistage interconnection networks under nonuniform traffic patterns. IEICE Transactions on Information and Systems (Special Issue on Architectures, Algorithms and Networks for Massively Parallel Computing) 79(8), 1124–1129 (1996)
4. Pfister, G.F., et al.: Hot spot contention and combining in multistage interconnection networks. IEEE Transactions on Computers 100(10), 943–948 (1985)

5. Phaal, P., et al.: InMon corporation's sFlow: A method for monitoring traffic in switched and routed networks. Technical report, RFC 3176 (2001)
6. Claise, B.: Cisco systems NetFlow services export version 9 (2004)
7. Case, J., et al.: A simple network management protocol (SNMP). In: Network Information Center, SRI International (1989)
8. IEEE: P802.1Qbb/D1.3 Virtual bridged local area networks - Amendment: Priority-based flow control. Technical report. IEEE (2010)
9. Mills, D., et al.: Network time protocol version 4: Protocol and algorithms specification (2010)
10. IEEE/ANSI: 1588 Standard for a precision clock synchronization protocol for networked measurement and control systems. Technical report, IEEE/ANSI (2008)
11. Kompella, R.R., et al.: Every microsecond counts: tracking fine-grain latencies with a lossy difference aggregator. In: ACM SIGCOMM CCR, vol. 39, pp. 255–266. ACM (2009)
12. Batraneanu, S., et al.: Operational model of the ATLAS TDAQ network. IEEE Transactions on Nuclear Science 55(2), 687–694 (2008)
13. Fisher, D., et al.: Using visualization to support network and application management in a data center. In: IEEE INM 2008, pp. 1–6 (2008)
14. Leiserson, C.E.: Fat-trees: universal networks for hardware-efficient supercomputing. IEEE Transactions on Computers 100(10), 892–901 (1985)
15. Petrini, F., et al.: Performance evaluation of the Quadrics interconnection network. Cluster Computing 6(2), 125–142 (2003)
16. Ohring, S.R., et al.: On generalized fat trees. In: Parallel Processing Symposium, pp. 37–44. IEEE (1995)
17. Dally, W., et al.: Principles and practices of interconnection networks. Morgan Kaufmann Publishers Inc., San Francisco (2003)
18. Minkenberg, C., et al.: Trace-driven co-simulation of high-performance computing systems using OMNeT++. In: SIMUTools 2009, p. 65 (2009)
19. Crisan, D., et al.: Short and Fat: TCP performance in CEE datacenter networks. In: HOTI 2011, pp. 43–50 (2011)
20. Gusat, M., et al.: R3C2: Reactive route and rate control for CEE. In: HOTI 2010, pp. 50–57 (2010)
21. Ferrari, P., et al.: Synchronization of the probes of a distributed instrument for real-time Ethernet networks. In: ISPCS 2007, pp. 33–40 (2007)
22. Correll, K.: et al.: Design considerations for software only implementations of the IEEE 1588 precision time protocol. In: Conference on IEEE 1588 Standard, vol. 1588, pp. 11–15 (2005)

Aggregation of Statistical Data from Passive Probes: Techniques and Best Practices

Silvia Colabrese[1], Dario Rossi[1], and Marco Mellia[2]

[1] Telecom ParisTech, Paris, France
{silvia.colabrese,dario.rossi}@enst.fr
[2] Politecnico di Torino, Torino, Italy
marco.mellia@polito.it

Abstract. Passive probes continuously generate statistics on large number of metrics, that are possibly represented as probability mass functions (pmf). The need for consolidation of several pmfs arises in two contexts, namely: (i) whenever a central point collects and aggregates measurement of multiple disjoint vantage points, and (ii) whenever a local measurement processed at a single vantage point needs to be distributed over multiple cores of the same physical probe, in order to cope with growing link capacity.

In this work, we take an experimental approach and study both cases using, whenever possible, open source software and datasets. Considering different consolidation strategies, we assess their accuracy in estimating pmf deciles (from the 10th to the 90th) of diverse metrics, obtaining general design and tuning guidelines. In our dataset, we find that Monotonic Spline Interpolation over a larger set of percentiles (e.g., adding 5th, 10th, 15th, and so on) allow fairly accurate pmf consolidation in both the multiple vantage points (median error is about 1%, maximum 30%) and local processes (median 0.1%, maximum 1%) cases.

1 Introduction

Passive probes collect a significant amount of traffic volume, and perform statistical analysis in a completely automated fashion. Very common statistical outputs include, from the coarsest to the finest grain: raw counts, averages, standard deviations, higher moments, percentiles and probability mass functions (pmf). Usually, computations are done locally at a probe, though there may be cases where the need for consolidation of multiple statistics, in a scalable and efficient way, arise.

We would now like to mention two completely orthogonal scenarios where this need arises, which we describe with the help of Fig. 1. In the figure, a number of *monitors* (denoted with an eye) generate statistics that are fed to a *collector* (denoted with gears) for consolidation. The figure further annotates the amount of traffic to be analyzed that flows across each monitored link.

First, in case of multiple vantage points of Fig. 1-(a), consolidation of several data sources is desirable as it yields a more statistically representative population sample. In cases where these probes are placed at PoP up in the network hierarchy, a limited number of M monitors suffices in gathering statistics representative of a large user population. However, in cases where probes represent individual house-holds, the number

A. Dainotti, A. Mahanti, and S. Uhlig (Eds.): TMA 2014, LNCS 8406, pp. 38–50, 2014.

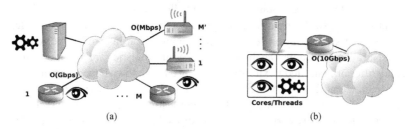

Fig. 1. Consolidation scenarios: statistical data is either produced by (a) multiple physically disjoint probes (heterogeneous traffic), or (b) a single multi-threaded probe (homogeneous traffic)

of M' monitors possibly grows much larger. As monitors and collector are physically disjoint, statistics have to be transferred to the collector – a potential system bottleneck.

Second, even in the case of a single vantage point of Fig. 1-(b), due to the sheer amount of traffic volume, it may be necessary to split traffic processing over multiple independent cores. Considering a high-end off-the-shelf multi-core architecture, the number of available CPUs limits the number of parallel processes to a few handful (we are not considering, at this stage, GPU-based architectures). In contrast to the previous case, monitors and collector are in this case colocated – so that processing power, rather than transfer of statistical data, becomes a potential system bottleneck.

While these two scenarios seem rather different at first sight, we argue that they translate into similar constraints. Thus we suggest using a single, flexible methodology to cope with both cases. In the case of multiple vantage points, using the least possible amount of statistical data is desirable to avoid a transfer bottleneck. In the case of parallel processing at a single vantage point, elaborating the least possible amount of data is desirable to limit the computational overhead tied to the consolidation process.

The above constraints possibly trade-off with the amount of data that is required to meet the desired accuracy level in the consolidation process, which additionally depends on the specific statistic of interest. Whenever the statistic X to be consolidated has the coarsest (i.e., count, averages or second moment) or finest (full pmf) grain, then the full set $\{X_j\}_{i=j}^M$ of statistics gathered over all M vantage points is needed for the consolidation process: the consolidation process then trivially combines these affine inputs (e.g., averaging the average, or maximum over all maximums, or summing the pmf frequency counters), weighting them on the ground of the amount of traffic T_i that each vantage point represents $w_i = T_i / \sum_{j=1}^M T_j$.

Instead, consolidation of intermediate-grain statistics, such as higher moments or quantiles of the distribution, raises a more interesting and challenging problem. For example, consider the problem of accurate estimation of the 90th percentile of a given metric, and assume for the sake of simplicity that all vantage points correspond to the same amount of traffic (i.e., unit weights $w_i = 1 \forall i$). It is clear that, while the fine grained knowledge of the pmf at all vantage points is not necessary to estimate the 90th percentiles of the aggregate pmf, the mere knowledge of the 90th percentiles over all vantage points is not sufficient.

While our aim is to propose a general methodology, and to obtain general design and tuning guidelines, in this paper we report on a specific instance of metrics gathered through the Tstat [1] measurement tool, a passive flow-level monitor that we developed over the last years [8]. We point out that, as other tools, Tstat produces both detailed flow-level logs at several layers (e.g, transport, application) as well as periodic statistics, stored as a Round Robin Database (RRD). While statistics are automatically computed, they offer only limited flexibility providing a breakdown depending on the traffic direction (e.g., client-2-server vs server-2-client, incoming vs outgoing). Hence, while aggregate statistics are useful, as they offer a long-lasting automatic of several networks indicator, in order to study correlation or conditioned probabilities across metrics, logs are ultimately needed. As such, consolidation of automatic statistics possibly tolerate slight inaccuracies if that provides sizable savings in terms of computational power or bandwidth.

In this paper, we focus on the estimation of pmf deciles (from the 10th to the 90th), considering vantage points located into rather different networks (open dataset whenever possible) and a large span of metrics (at IP, TCP and UDP layer). We employ different consolidation strategies (e.g., Linear vs Spline interpolation techniques) and a varying amount of information (i.e., considering the deciles, or also additional quantiles of the distribution). In the remainder of this paper, we outline the methodology (Sec. 2) and dataset (Sec. 3) we follow in our experimental campaign (Sec. 4). A discussion of related work (Sec. 5) and guidelines (Sec. 6) concludes the paper.

2 Methodology

2.1 Features

The most concise way to represent a pmf or the related distribution is by the use of percentiles. Tstat computes two kinds of percentiles:

Per-flow percentiles. For these fine-grained metrics, Tstat employs an online technique based on constant-space data structures (namely, PSquare [13]): percentiles of per-flow metrics are then stored in flow-level logs. Though PSquare is very efficient in both computational complexity and memory footprint (namely, requiring only 5 counters per percentile), due to the large number of flows it is only seldom used (e.g., to measure 90th, 95th and 99th percent of queuing delay to measure bufferbloat [5]).

Aggregated percentiles. For this coarse grain metric, Tstat employs standard fixed-width histograms: percentiles of the distribution are then evaluated with linear interpolation, and stored in Round Robin Databases (RRD). Generally, each flow contributes one sample to the aggregate distribution, and several breakdowns of the whole aggregated are automatically generated depending on the traffic direction (e.g., client-2-server vs server-2-client, incoming vs outgoing).

For reasons of space, we are unable to report the full list of traffic features tracked by Tstat as aggregate metrics (for a detailed description, we refer the reader to [1]). We point out that these span multiple layers, from network (i.e., IP) to transport (i.e., TCP, UDP, RTP) and application layers (e.g., Skype, HTTP, YouTube). Since not all kinds of traffic are available across all traces (e.g., no Skype or multimedia traffic is present in the oldest trace in our dataset), we only consider the IP, TCP and UDP metrics.

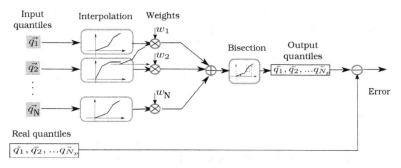

Fig. 2. Synopsis of the experimental workflow

2.2 Consolidation Workflow

In this work, we focus on the coarse-grain dataset and estimate *quantiles* of the distribution. We describe our workflow with the help of Fig. 2, considering a generic traffic feature. Shaded gray blocks are the input to our system. Such blocks represent quantiles vectors q_i, gathered from multiple (local or remote) Tstat probes running at location i, with $i \in [1, N_P]$. We *interpolate* each quantile vector to get a cumulative distribution function (CDF). These functions are weighted by the amount of traffic they represent (weights can be computed in terms of flows, packets or bytes), and added to get the total CDF. Finally, as output of our workflow, we obtain the consolidated $\overline{q}_i$ deciles vector from the total CDF with the bisection method.

It is worth noticing that the procedure implicitly yields *continuous* CDF functions, whereas the empirical CDFs computed through Tstat histograms are *piecewise constant* functions instead. To cope with this, it would be possible to quantize a posteriori the gathered quantiles for discrete variables (e.g., packet length, IP TTL). However, we neglect this step because (i) we aim for a fully automated process, whereas this per-feature optimization would require manual intervention and (ii) we expect the impact due to missed rounding of integer values to be minor anyway.

Finally, the consolidated continuous output is compared to the real quantiles $\overline{q}_i$ of the aggregated distribution, obtained from running Tstat on the aggregated traces. In what follows, we evaluate the accuracy of the overall workflow via the relative error $err_i = (\overline{q}_i - \tilde{q}_i)/\tilde{q}_i$ of the consolidation process.

2.3 Interpolation

To obtain the CDFs, we employ two kinds of interpolation.

Linear (L). For each couple of consecutive deciles, linear interpolation reconstructs the CDF by using an affine equation $y = mx + q$. Being (q_i, p_i) and (q_{i+1}, p_{i+1}) the given points, $m = \frac{p_{i+1} - p_i}{q_{i+1} - q_i}$ and $q = p_i$. If the function to approximate were continuous in both their first and second derivative (i.e., $f \in C^2$) then we could upper bound the error through the Rolle's Theorem. Yet, these assumptions do not hold in the majority of real cases, so that we can just expect that, the steeper the first derivative, the higher the errors.

Monotonic Spline (S). Cubic Splines are Piecewise polynomial functions with $n = 3$. Given that $CDF(a) \leq CDF(b)$ when $a \leq b$ we need to ensure the monotonicity of the data. This constraint is met employing the Piecewise Cubic Hermite Interpolating Polynomial [9]. The obtained polynomial is $\in C^1$: i.e., the first derivative is continuous, whereas continuity of the second derivative is not guaranteed.

2.4   Input vs Output

As output, we are interested in evaluating all *deciles* of the distribution: along with minimum and maximum values, these represent compact summaries of the whole CDF. Our methodology exploits quantiles to reconstruct the distributions, and operate over CDFs. In principle, this allows to gather any set of output quantiles from CDFs reconstructed from a set of different input quantiles. In this work, we consider two cases:

Single (S). In the simplest case, we consider *deciles* as both input and output of our workflow.

Double (D). We argue that CDF interpolation can benefit from a larger number of samples (i.e., knots in Spline terms), providing a more accurate description for the intermediate consolidation process. As such, we additionally consider the possibility of using additional intermediate (i.e., 5th, 15th, 25th to 95th) quantiles of the distribution (i.e., that carry a double amount of information with respect to the previous case).

While the above two scenarios are not fully representative of the whole input vs output space (where in principle the full cross-product of input vs output quantiles sets could be considered) however, we point out that they already provide insights about the value of additional input information. We expect these settings to quantify the relative importance of information available at the ingress of the system, with respect to the specific methodology used for, e.g., interpolation in the workflow.

3   Datasets

We use several traces, some of which are publicly available. Vantage points pertain to different network environments (e.g., Campus and ISP networks), countries (e.g., EU and Australia) and have been collected over a period of over 8 years. This extreme heterogeneity attempts to obtain conservative accuracy values: our expectation is that, as not only the environment and the geography largely differ, but also since the traffic patterns, application mixtures and Internet infrastructure have evolved, this setup should be significantly more challenging than a typical use case. In more details, traces refer to:

Campus. Captured during 2009 at University of Brescia (UniBS), this publicly available trace [3] is representative of a typical data connection to the Internet. LAN users can be administrative, faculty members and students.

Table 1. Summary of dataset used in this work

Trace	ISP	Campus	Auckland-VI
Year	2006	2008	2001
Packets	44,396,297	17,246,459	291,052,998
Flows	219,481	422,928	11,128,910
Packets/flow	202.27	40.77	26.15
IPs	61,959	81,687	410,059

ISP. Collected during 2006 from one of the major European ISP, which we cannot cite due to NDA, offering triple-play services (Voice, Video/TV, Data) over broadband access. ISP is representative of a very heterogeneous scenario, in which no traffic restriction are applied to customers.

Auckland. Captured during 2001 at the Internet egress router of the University of Auckland, this publicly available trace [2] enlarges the traffic mix and temporal span of our dataset.

While we are unable to report details of the above dataset for lack of space, we point out that these are available at the respective sites [2, 3], of which we additionally provide statistics on [16]. To simplify our analysis, we consider a subset of about 200,000 randomly sampled flows for each trace[1], which implies equal weights. Given that each flow represents a sample for the CDF, we observe that CDFs are computed over a statistically significant population.

4 Experiments

4.1 Scenario and Settings

Starting from the above dataset, we construct two consolidation scenarios: for the local parallel processing case (*Homogeneous*), we uniformly sample flows from the ISP trace, that we split into $N \in [2, 8]$ subtraces (in the $N = 8$ case, the population accounts to about 25,000 flows for each individual CDF). For the multiple remote vantage points case (*Heterogeneous*), we instead consider the three traces (about 600,000 flows).

To give a simple example of the variability of metrics we report in Fig. 3 the distribution of an IP-level (i.e., IP packet length) metric in the parallel processing (left) and multiple vantage point (right) scenarios. As expected, differences in the parallel processing case are minor: as sampling is uniform, each of the N subsamples already yields a good estimate of the overall aggregate distribution. Conversely, significant differences appear in the multiple vantage points scenario: in this case, the application mixture impacting the relative frequency of packet sizes (e.g., 0-payload ACK vs small-size VoIP packets vs full-size frames data packets) has significantly evolved[2].

---

[1] Actually, we consider the full ISP trace, so sample size is 219,481 flows for each trace.

[2] Additionally, changes in the MTU size due to Operating System and Internet infrastructure evolution are possible causes, that would however need further verification.

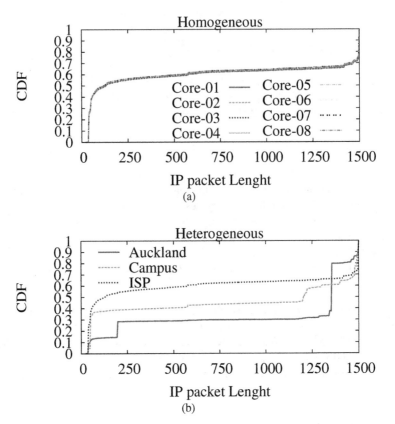

Fig. 3. Example of variation of an IP-level metric (i.e., IP packet length) in (a) Homogeneous vs (b) Heterogeneous settings

Overall, we consider four consolidation settings, arising from different combination of interpolation techniques and inputs, namely: Linear Simple (LS), Linear Double (LD), Spline Simple (SS), Spline Double (SD) – that correspond to different computational complexity and data amount settings. Our aim is to assess the extent of accuracy gains that can be gathered through the use of more complex interpolation techniques, or through the exchange of a larger amount of information.

4.2   Methodology Tuning

We first assess the consolidation accuracy in the LS, LD, SS, SD settings, for both homogeneous and heterogeneous scenarios. We report the average error (with standard deviation bars) in Fig. 4. The plot is additionally annotated with the accuracy gain over the naive LS setting.

First, notice that in the homogeneous scenario the error is very low, but grows of about two orders of magnitude in our heterogeneous one (where all techniques are

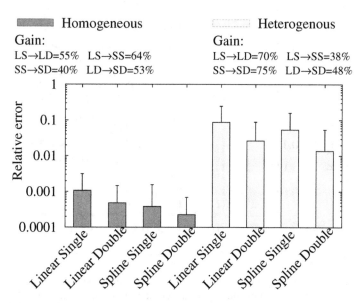

Fig. 4. Methodology tuning: Consolidation error in the Linear vs Spline, Single vs Double case for the IP TTL metric considering Homogeneous and Heterogeneous cases

largely ineffective). Second, it can be seen that while Spline interpolation has an important impact (at least 38%), doubling the amount of quantiles however has an ever higher impact. Moreover, this is especially true in the more difficult heterogeneous scenario, where gains are in excess of 70% when interpolation happens over a denser set of quantiles, whereas Spline interpolation gain at most 48%. While this is an interesting observation, it raises an important question, which we leave for future research: namely, to precisely assess in which conditions, over all metrics and input-output possibilities, having a larger amount of information is more beneficial than employing more sophisticated interpolation techniques.

As a consequence, in what follows we limitedly consider the SD setting (i.e., Spline interpolation over Double set of quantiles), as it yields to the best consolidation results.

4.3 Breakdown

Next, we show a per-percentile per-metric breakdown of the relative error in Fig. 5. For the sake of illustration, we consider a few metrics that are representative of different layers (IP, TCP, UDP). To get conservative results, we consider only the most challenging heterogeneous scenario. As it can be expected, errors are not tied to a particular decile, as the error is rather tied to the steepness of the change in the CDF around that decile for that particular metric. For example, considering the IP packet length metric, due to significant CDF differences across traces depicted early in Fig. 3-(b), it can be expected that deciles below the median are hard to consolidate: this is reflected by large errors for the corresponding deciles in Fig. 5.

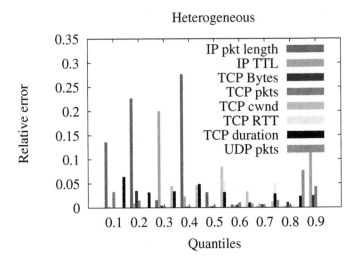

Fig. 5. Methodology tuning: Breakdown of relative error under the Spline Double consolidation strategy for different percentiles and metrics under the Heterogeneous case

As we previously have observed, rather than trying harder to correct these estimation errors a posteriori (i.e., using Spline instead of Linear interpolation), greater accuracy is expected to come only at a price of a larger amount of information (i.e., quantiles for CDF interpolation), and are ultimately tied to the size of the binning strategy in Tstat.

Otherwise stated, our recommendation is to selectively bias the amount of quantiles: instead of indiscriminately increasing the amount of quantiles for all metrics, one could use denser quantiles (or finer binning) only for metrics with a high subjective value in the scenario under investigation. This could be facilitated by a integer "overfit" factor extending beyond the values Simple($=1$), Double ($=2$) explored in this work, that could be easily set during an initial probe configuration phase.

4.4 Homogeneous vs Heterogeneous

We now report a complete CDF of the relative error over all Tstat metrics and percentiles in Fig. 6, where we compare the heterogeneous and homogeneous case (to get a fair comparison, we consider only $N = 3$ subsets in both cases). As previously observed, there is a sizable difference in terms of accuracy, with median relative error in the homogeneous (heterogeneous) cases of 0.1% (1%), and maximum error of 1% (30%). Notice that we are considering Spline with Double quantiles, otherwise errors in the heterogeneous settings could grow even further. It follows that, while the consolidation appears to be rather robust in homogeneous settings, it may serve as a mere visual indication depending on the specific metric and decile (recall Fig. 5), but cannot otherwise be considered reliable (or, at least, a calibration phase is needed in to assess the relative error with any different set of remote vantage points).

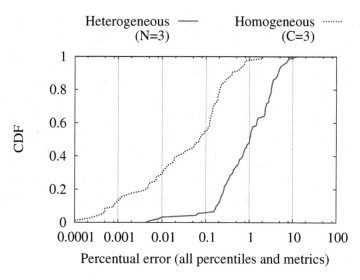

Fig. 6. Accuracy of Double Spline consolidation strategy: CDF of relative error, all metrics and deciles, in the homogeneous vs heterogeneous scenarios

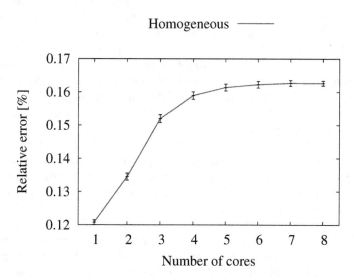

Fig. 7. Accuracy of Double Spline consolidation strategy: Average relative error for varying number of cores N in the homogeneous scenario

4.5   Parallel Local Probes

Finally, we verify the effect of splitting the trace in an arbitrary number of parallel processes: we do so by artificially splitting the ISP trace into multiple $N \in [2, 8]$ subtraces, and process them independently. In principle, it would be desirable to use an arbitrarily high number of cores, as this would allow the monitoring tool scale with the link load. At the same time, we expect consolidation accuracy to decrease with growing N, so that an empirical assessment of its error is mandatory, so to gauge to what extent parallelization could compromise the accuracy of the statistical results. Results are reported in Fig. 7 averaged over all metrics (bars report this time the error variance, as the standard deviation of a number $e \in [0, 1]$ produce otherwise a too large visual noise). It can be seen that the error[3], though very limited for any $N > 1$, grows logarithmically with N. This implies that the largest accuracy loss happens whenever a monolithic process is split into 2-3 parallel processes, suggesting that a monitoring tool can safely scale to N cores.

5   Related Work

Statistical data processing and aggregation in distributed systems is surely not a novel research field. Yet, in the telecommunication network domain, the problem has so far been treated in rather different settings (e.g., sensor vs peer-to-peer networks) with respect to ours.

From a system level, this is easily understood since only very recent work offered high-speed packet capture libraries [4, 10, 17] enabling parallel processing of network traffic. Work such as [10] or [6] leverage this possibility for packet forwarding or traffic classification respectively, though work that focuses on traffic monitoring is closer to ours [7, 12, 15]. For example, [7] focus on making log storage cope with line rate, deferring the process of analysis and consolidation as a offline process. Other recent work defines fully-fledged frameworks for distributed processing [12, 15]. While these systems have merits, they are far more general than the issue studied in this work. Yet performance analysis is limited to show-case functionality of the tools, though neither practical algorithms nor guidelines are given for our problem at hand.

In the distributed system settings, generally the focus has been on either (i) compact and efficient algorithms and data structures for quantile estimation, or on (ii) protocols to compute an estimate of the entire distribution in a decentralized and efficient manner. As for (i), among the various techniques, a particular mention goes to the PSquare method [13], that is still considered as the state of the art [14, 18], and is implemented in Tstat. As for (ii), [11] proposes a gossip protocol to distribute computation of Equi-Width and Equi-Depth histograms, evaluating the convergence speed (measured in number of rounds) and quality (Kolmogorov-Smirov distance between the actual and estimated distributions). In our case, a single collector point allow us to minimize the communication overhead and perform consolidation in a single round. More recently,

---

[3] Baseline error for $N = 1$ represent the error tied to fixed-width binning and linear interpolation for percentile estimation implemented in Tstat, as opposite to state of the art techniques for accurate percentile estimation based on variable width binning.

a number of approaches are compared in [19], that would be interesting to adapt and specialize to our settings.

Finally, it is worth mentioning that this problem is orthogonal to the widely used technique of traffic sampling, with which the techniques considered in this work are furthermore inter-operable. Indeed, traffic sampling (e.g., at flow level) is useful in reducing the sheer volume of traffic flows that have to be processed at a single probe; yet, flow sampling does not affect the volume of statistical data that is produced by the monitors, and that is ultimately fed to collectors. Recalling our use cases, flow sampling may relieve CPU bottlenecks of the multi-process case of Fig. 1-(b), but it does otherwise not affect the amount of statistical data reaching the collector in Fig. 1-(a). To this latter end, a spatial sampling among monitors could reduce the amount of statistical data fed to the collector, though this could tradeoff with the representativeness of the data – an interesting question that deserves further attention.

6   Conclusions

In this work we address the problem of consolidating statistical properties of network monitoring tools coming from multiple probes, either as a result of parallel processing at a single vantage point, or collected from multiple vantage points. Summarizing our contributions, we find that:

- as it can be expected, while consolidation error is practically negligible in the case of local processes, where statistics are more similar across cores (median error is about 0.1% and maximum 1%), it is however possibly rather large in the case of multiple disjoint vantage points with diverse traffic natures (median error is about 1% and maximum 30%, though it possibly exceeds 100% for naive strategies);
- the use of intermediate pmf quantiles (e.g., 5th, 15th, and so on), is desirable as it significantly improves accuracy (up to 75% in the case of multiple vantage points), even though it tradeoffs with communication and computational complexity;
- interpolation via Splines is preferable over simpler Linear interpolation, as it yields to an accuracy gain of over 40% in our dataset;
- the error in case of parallel processing grows logarithmically with the number of processes, suggesting parallel processing tools to be a viable way to cope with growing link capacity at the price of a tolerable accuracy loss.

As part of our ongoing work, we are building this consolidation system as a general tool, able to work on RRD databases. We also plan to extend our analysis of the accuracy to cover a larger set of input vs output features (i.e., quantiles or other properties) combination, and to more systematically analyze benefits of interpolation vs additional information in these broader settings.

Acknowledgement. This work has been carried out at LINCS http://www.lincs .fr and funded by EU under FP7 Grant Agreement no. 318627 (Integrated project "mPlane").

References

1. http://tstat.tlc.polito.it
2. Auckland traces, http://www.wand.net.nz/
3. Unibs traces, http://www.ing.unibs.it/ntw/tools/traces/
4. Bonelli, N., Pietro, A.D., Giordano, S., Procissi, G.: Pfq: a novel engine for multi-gigabit packet capturing with multi-core commodity hardware. In: Taft, N., Ricciato, F. (eds.) PAM 2012. LNCS, vol. 7192, pp. 64–73. Springer, Heidelberg (2012)
5. Chirichella, C., Rossi, D.: To the moon and back: are internet bufferbloat delays really that large. In: IEEE INFOCOM Workshop on Traffic Measurement and Analysis, TMA (2013)
6. del Rio, P.S., Rossi, D., Gringoli, F., Nava, L.S.L., Aracil, J.: Wire-speed statistical classification of network traffic on commodity hardware. In: ACM SIGCOMM Internet Measurement Conference, IMC (2012)
7. Deri, L., Cardigliano, A., Fusco, F.: 10 gbit line rate packet-to-disk using n2disk. In: IEEE INFOCOM Workshop on Traffic Monitoring and Analysis, TMA (2013)
8. Finamore, A., Mellia, M., Meo, M., Munafo, M., Rossi, D.: Experiences of internet traffic monitoring with tstat. IEEE Network (2011)
9. Fritsch, F.N., Carlson, R.E.: Monotone piecewise cubic interpolation. SIAM Journal on Numerical Analysis 17(2), 238–246 (1980)
10. Han, S., Jang, K., Park, K., Moon, S.: Packetshader: a gpu-accelerated software router. In: ACM SIGCOMM (2010)
11. Haridasan, M., van Renesse, R.: Gossip-based distribution estimation in peer-to-peer networks. In: USENIX Internet Peer-to-Peer Symposium, IPTPS (2008)
12. Huici, F., Di Pietro, A., Trammell, B., Gomez Hidalgo, J.M., Martinez Ruiz, D., d'Heureuse, N.: Blockmon: A high-performance composable network traffic measurement system. ACM SIGCOMM Computer Communication Review 42(4), 79–80 (2012)
13. Jain, R., Chlamtac, I.: The p^2 algorithm for dynamic calculation of quantiles and histograms without storing observations. Communications of the ACM 28(10), 1076–1085 (1985)
14. Kilpi, J., Varjonen, S.: Minimizing information loss in sequential estimation of several quantiles. Technical Report (2009)
15. Lyra, C., Hara, C.S., Duarte Jr., E.P.: BackStreamDB: A distributed system for backbone traffic monitoring providing arbitrary measurements in real-time. In: Taft, N., Ricciato, F. (eds.) PAM 2012. LNCS, vol. 7192, pp. 42–52. Springer, Heidelberg (2012)
16. Pescape, A., Rossi, D., Tammaro, D., Valenti, S.: On the impact of sampling on traffic monitoring and analysis. In: International Teletraffic Congress, ITC22 (2010)
17. Rizzo, L.: Revisiting network i/o apis: the netmap framework. Commun. ACM 55(3), 45–51 (2012)
18. Wang, H., Ciucu, F., Schmitt, J.: A leftover service curve approach to analyze demultiplexing in queueing networks. In: VALUETOOLS (2012)
19. Wang, L., Luo, G., Yi, K., Cormode, G.: Quantiles over data streams: an experimental study. In: ACM SIGMOD (2013)

Characterizing Bufferbloat
and Its Impact at End-Hosts

Stéphane Wustner[1,2], Renata Teixeira[3], and Jaideep Chandrashekar[2]

[1] UPMC Sorbonne Universities, Paris, France
[2] Technicolor, Paris, France
[3] Inria, France

Abstract. While buffers on forwarding devices are required to handle bursty Internet traffic, overly large or badly sized buffers can interact with TCP in undesirable ways. This phenomenon is well understood and is often called "bufferbloat". Although a number of previous studies have shown that buffering (particularly, in home) can delay packets by as much as a few seconds in the worst case, there is less empirical evidence of tangible impacts on end-users. In this paper, we develop a modified algorithm that can detect bufferbloat at individual end-hosts based on passive observations of traffic. We then apply this algorithm on packet traces collected at 55 end-hosts, and across different network environments. Our results show that 45 out of the 55 users we study experience bufferbloat at least once, 40% of these users experience bufferbloat more than once per hour. In 90% of cases, buffering more than doubles RTTs, but RTTs during bufferbloat are rarely over one second. We also show that web and interactive applications, which are particularly sensitive to delay, are the applications most often affected by bufferbloat.

1 Introduction

Internet routers and other forwarding devices (e.g., home gateways, midddbleboxes) are engineered with buffers that can help deal with sudden bursts in traffic. When properly sized, these buffers can avoid packet losses which could lead to network instability. However, on the other hand, large buffers can interact with TCP's feedback control mechanism in unexpected ways. Such buffers have the effect of *delaying* TCP feedback, making the end-points wait longer to understand the fate of packets that are in flight. Recent papers report that excessive buffering at the edge (mostly in home routers and access points) can cause additional delay on the order of seconds [1], as a direct result of what is termed *BufferBloat* [2,3]. When buffering is excessive, and the delays large, applications seem "laggier" and end-users perceive the network as being slower and less responsive. Such effects are most felt with short interactive (or semi-interactive) applications such as web-browsing, VoIP, and online gaming.

Most previous work in this area has focused on two distinct aspects: (i) measuring the extent of excessive buffering in the network, or (ii) designing mechanisms to mitigate it. Corresponding to the first category, previous work quantifies

A. Dainotti, A. Mahanti, and S. Uhlig (Eds.): TMA 2014, LNCS 8406, pp. 51–64, 2014.

worst case buffering carrying out delay measurements after attempting to satu-
rate network buffer [1] [4] [5], or leveraging bittorent traffic [6]. This body of work
conclusively establishes that bufferbloat can occur on the Internet for a particular set of conditions. However, they do not address the question of whether this
directly affects the normal user (and their traffic) and to what extent. The one
exception to this is the work by Allman [7], which analyzed real user traffic seen
deep in the network and reported that bufferbloat rarely delays packets by more
than a second (which contrasts some of the previous work). A possible explanation is that the dataset consists primarily of fiber users with 1GB bi-directional
links, and the lack of buffering is simply due to the very high access link speeds.

In this paper, we examine a different vantage point to characterize the size
and impact of excessive buffering, and this is on the end-host itself. By placing
ourselves *on* the end-host, we are better able to measure and understand the act
ual performance of an application *as experienced by the end-user*. It is extremely
challenging to close the loop and actually state whether a bad performance
episode indeed has an impact on the user – such observations are very subjective and depend on application, mood, expectations, etc. In our work, we simply
measure how some application characteristics are degraded by excessive buffering, which serves as a proxy for the actual experience of the end-user. Another
advantage of being able to characterize this at the end-host is that mechanisms
might be easier to deploy at the end-hosts and the mitigation mechanisms, such
as those discussed in [8,9] could be customized for particular applications. A
key challenge that needs to be addressed is a methodology to detect excessive
buffering, which intimately depends on a large set of parameters – access link
speeds, buffer sizes, traffic rates, etc. This has been narrowly addressed in previous work [3], which was squarely focused on the network core. However, these
methods are not directly applicable at the end-host.

A key contribution of this paper is a modified algorithm that can detect
extended periods of buffering passively and on end-hosts.

Subsequently, we apply this new detection methodology on a corpus of data
(described in §2) collected from 55 hosts, covering 2300 cumulative days of traffic.
The users and environments in our dataset cover a wide variety of network
settings – ranging from enterprise LAN networks to home DSL networks. Our
characterization (§4) complements Allman's study [7], which only examined very
well connected end-hosts. In particular, we focus onto individual bufferbloat
episodes and quantify the *actual* impact on applications that are affected by the
buffering in the particular episode.

2   Dataset

We study bufferbloat using data passively collected directly on users' machines
with the Hostview [10] monitoring tool. HostView was developed to study user
perception of network performance. It collects network and system performance
as well as user feedback on the quality of network experience. In this paper, we
only study the network performance of active application connections. HostView

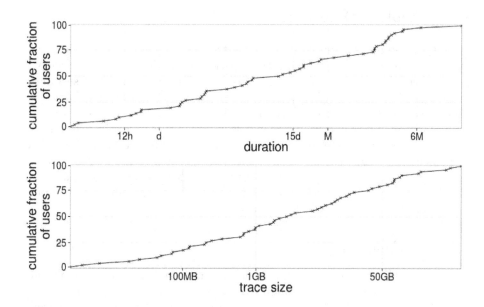

Fig. 1. Distribution of the duration covered by capture across users

extracts network performance from packet-header traces collected with libpcap. It labels traces with information about the network *environment*: (i) the hash of the MAC address of the default gateway, (ii) the interface name, (iii) the type of the interface. HostView uploads traces from the user machine to a server every four hours. We merge all consecutive traces collected in a single environment collected less than one hour apart into a *session*. We then process packets in each session with tcptrace [11] to obtain round-trip time (RTT) estimates over each TCP connection in the session. Note that because the data is collected at the end-host we can only estimate RTTs for upload traffic and at the beginning and end of every connection (since the RTT estimations relies on ACKs). This is not a problem for our study because bufferbloat has mainly been observed in upload traffic [1] [4] [5]. HostView also maps connections to the application executable name that originated them using GT [12]. This allows us to identify the application running within particular intervals.

Users, mostly computer scientists, ran HostView between November 2010 and April 2012. We study data from 55 users who contributed at least four hours of cumulative trace over ethernet. We only study traces collected when users are connected over Ethernet to avoid any interaction with other buffering effects happening in wireless. The traces we study were collected on 87 unique network environments in 14 different countries. The sizes of traces and the duration varied per user as we can see in Figure 1. We study traces that lasted between 4 hours and 15 months, depending on the user. For 80% of users the traces lasted for at least one day. Trace sizes also vary considerably across users; the median trace is 2.6GB.

3   Bufferbloat Detection

Given RTT samples computed from packet traces collected on the end-host, we must detect periods when packets are experiencing bufferbloat. We develop a methodology that works in two steps. First, we identify instances of sustained buffering, which we call *buffering episodes*, using a heuristic inspired by *coDel* [3]. Then, we apply this heuristic to the HostView data to identify episodes of excessive buffering and quantify their magnitude. From these, we select the largest episodes and analyze them in detail. This section first presents a brief overview of the heuristic coDel uses to detect buffering, then it presents how we extend this heuristic to work only with the data that we have available at end-hosts. Finally, we present our analysis of buffering on HostView data and the definition of bufferbloat we will consider for the rest of the paper.

3.1   CoDel Heuristic

CoDel is an active queue management algorithm designed for gateways. The algorithm detects when queue is building up so that it can start dropping packets early, to avoid *bufferbloat*. As a basis to our detector we choose the same, well-tested, heuristics as in coDel. CoDel measures the sojourn time at the buffer. It declares a buffering episode when the sojourn time is above a *target* for at least an *interval* (in the original work, these are set as 5ms and 100ms, respectively [3]). These two heuristics are complementary: a sojourn time greater than a certain target would not necessarily imply there is a buffering episode, while a sojourn time sustained above that target and over a large interval implies the phenomenon was not transient.

3.2   Detecting of Buffering Episodes at End-Hosts

The coDel heuristic doesn't apply *directly* at end-hosts: (i) we need to estimate the sojourn time from RTT samples, which can suffer from measurement noise mostly due to traffic conditions; (ii) in addition, we only observe traffic from one of the end-hosts behind the buffer (if the applications running on the end-host are not sending traffic continuously, which is often the case in practice, then we may not have enough samples to determine whether the additional delay in the buffer was indeed sustained for at least the given interval). We propose the following modification to the coDel heuristic to address these issues.

Additional Delay as an Estimate of Sojourn Time. We use the *additional delay* of an RTT sample computed as the RTT sample minus the baseline latency to the same destination as an estimator for sojourn time across all buffers along the path (we assume that, only one hop is experiencing a buffering episode at a time). To estimate the baseline latency to a destination we select the minimum RTT we observe for that destination during a session. Our algorithm later verifies whether a baseline latency estimate was computed during a buffering episode.

If so, then we cannot be confident in our estimate of additional delay. If the additional delay is above the target, then we can still consider this sample. Otherwise, we discard the sample.

Setting Target and Interval. We set the target to 5ms and the interval to 100ms as in coDel [3]. Although we are measuring additional delay at end-hosts and not the sojourn time in the buffer of the router, we choose to be conservative and use the same parameters as coDel. We will later filter out these episodes to select just the largest episodes (which we would have also detected using a higher target, or a longer interval).

Dealing with Measurement Noise. CoDel defines the end of an episode when the sojourn time falls back under the target. Measurement noise may cause some RTT samples to be below the target even though the end-host is still experiencing the same buffering episode. This may happen when we overestimate the baseline latency for some destinations. To avoid breaking up one long episode into multiple shorter episodes, we aggregate shorter episodes that are within a threshold time of each other into a larger episode. This threshold time is defined as the smoothed average additional delay of all samples in the first episode plus the baseline latency of the last sample of this episode. We use the smoothed average because tcptrace sometimes reports unrealistic high RTTs that we attribute to measurement noise.

Dealing with Sparsity of Samples. In some cases, the end-host we monitor may not be sending enough traffic, either because the application is not trying to send traffic or because buffering is so bad that sending rate becomes really low. If the problem is the latter, then we should see at least one sample per RTT. To account for these cases, we define that two RTT samples can potentially belong to the same episode if they are separated by less than a threshold. We set this threshold to the baseline latency of the last sample of this episode plus the smoothed average of the additional delay of this episode.

Gateway versus End-Host View. We then compare the output of our end-host heuristic with that of coDel running at the gateway with a controlled experiment using a simple topology: client—gateway—server. We vary uplink bandwidth from 10Kbps to 6Mbps and downlink bandwidth from 56Kbps to 100Mbps in both links; buffer size from 10 to 400 Kbits at the gateway; and latency from 5ms to 100ms and jitter from 1ms to 20ms at the server. Results vary depending on specific network conditions, but in general we see that: (i) the duration of episodes detected at the end-host is shorter than the duration of the same episode measured at the gateway (this is mainly due to the sparsity of samples), (ii) the additional delay seen at the end-host is most of the time larger than the sojourn time at the gateway (due to the effect of the jitter on tcp-trace's RTT calculation), (iii) the fraction of time where we detect a buffering

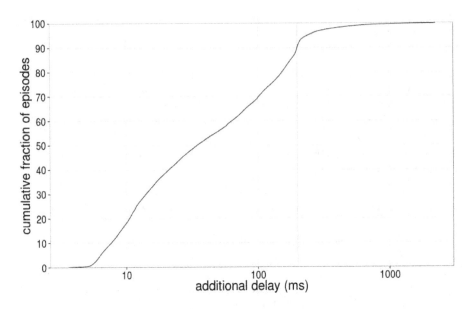

Fig. 2. Distribution of additional delay per buffering episode (computed as the area under the curve of additional delays of samples during this episode). We define all episodes that incur at least 200ms of additional delay as bufferbloat.

episode at the end-host and coDel also detects an episode is 60%. Note that these two vantage points are measuring different things and that there is no notion of ground truth here. This comparison is only useful to illustrate how the two metrics differ.

3.3   Identifying Bufferbloat

We apply the heuristic described in the previous section to the HostView data to identify the beginning and end of buffering episodes. Not all buffering episodes are significant, in fact most buffering is just part of normal TCP/network behavior. We now want to select a subset of the buffering episodes that are significant enough to potentially impact users. Figure 2 presents the cumulative distribution of the additional delay per episode (the x-axis is in log scale). We compute the *additional delay for an episode* using the area under the curve defined by the additional delay corresponding to the successive RTT samples within this episode. For this computation we only take into consideration samples for which the baseline latency was computed outside of an episode. The additional delay of buffering episodes in our data varies from 5ms (which is the value of the target) to over 22 seconds. This distribution has a sharp knee at 200ms. 90% of buffering episodes cause less than 200ms of additional delay. An additional delay of 200ms is significant when compared to typical RTTs and it should impact many interactive applications. Therefore, we choose to define *bufferbloat* as all buffering episodes that incur at least 200ms of additional delay. In the rest of this paper, we only study bufferbloated episodes.

Our approach allows us to infer the beginning and the end of each bufferbloat episode. This contrasts with Allman's study [7], which simply studies distributions of absolute RTTs and discusses how often RTTs larger than one second happen in the traces. Allman's approach is appealing because it avoids having to parametrize bufferbloat, which is challenging in practice. Nevertheless, we choose to detect bufferbloat episodes so that we can study their duration, their magnitude, and their impact on applications. We pick a conservative threshold empirically to focus only on the largest episodes.

4   Bufferbloat Characterization

This section analyzes bufferbloat episodes observed in the traffic of the 55 HostView users. We first study the occurrence of bufferbloat episodes and their duration. Then, we study by how much bufferbloat inflates RTTs and the duration of TCP connections. Finally, we analyze bufferbloat impact per application.

4.1   Bufferbloat Occurrence

We detect at least one bufferbloat episode for 45 out of the 55 users we studied. This result shows that bufferbloat affects users traffic in practice. Figure 3 presents the histogram of the number of bufferbloat episodes per hour for each of the 45 users who experienced at least one episode. We bin users according to the number of episodes per hour. For example, the first bin groups all users that had between zero and one episode per hour. Although the majority of users experienced less than one episode per hour, seven users experienced more than ten episodes per hour. One user, who connected from a residential ISP in Lebanon, experienced as many as 19.7 episodes per hour. We cannot generalize based on measurements from a single user. This example suggests, however, that having a larger deployment in developing regions, where residential access speeds are often lower, could discover a much higher occurrence of bufferbloat.

4.2   Duration of Bufferbloat Episodes

We study the duration of bufferbloat episodes. Intuitively, inflated RTTs over longer periods of time are more likely to affect users. Both the duration and the magnitude of bufferbloat episodes depend on the network environment users connect from: the size of the buffer, the connection speed (i.e., the buffer draining rate), and the usage patterns (i.e., the traffic demand at the buffer). Figure 4 presents the distribution of duration of bufferbloat episodes per environment. We observe bufferbloat in a total of 86 network environments, but we only present results for the 49 environments where we observed at least 100 bufferbloat episodes. We order environments by the median duration of episodes. In all the environments, the median episode duration is above 200ms. However, the median duration rarely exceeds 2s. We identify the ISP for the six environments with largest

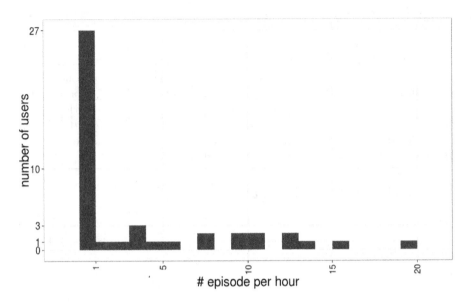

Fig. 3. Histogram of the number of episodes per hour across users. The ticks in the x-axis mark the end of the range in a bin. The first bin groups users from 0 to 1 bufferbloat episode per hour, whereas the last groups users between 19 and 20 episodes per hour.

median episode duration and find that most of them are residential providers (two of them are a campus network, which may in fact be students who are in on-campus housing). This result confirms Allman's findings that residential users often experience higher buffering delays than non-residential [7].

This figure shows that the duration of episodes vary considerably across environments and within an environment. Variation of episode duration across environments comes mainly from the differences in buffer size and connection speed, whereas variation in a single environment comes from the different traffic demands over time.

4.3   Impact of Bufferbloat Episodes

We now study the impact of bufferbloat episodes: how are connections affected? how are latencies and connection duration inflated? As in §3.3, we use the area under the curve of the additional delay of RTT samples in an episode as the additional delay of the episode. We already saw in the results presented in Figure 2 that the absolute value of additional delay for bufferbloat episodes vary from 200ms (which is how we define bufferbloat) to over 10s. However, 200ms of additional delay on a baseline RTT of 20ms is far more significant than on a baseline of 200ms. We define the *normalized additional delay* of an RTT sample as the additional delay of an episode divided by the baseline latency for each RTT sample in that episode.

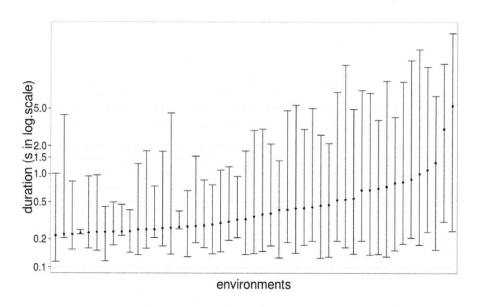

Fig. 4. Box-plot of the duration of bufferbloat episodes across network environments with more than 100 episodes (ordered by the median duration of bufferbloat episodes). The point in the middle represents the median episode duration for an environment; the bottom line represents the 5th-% and the upper line the 95th-%.

Figure 5 presents the cumulative distribution of the median normalized additional delay of RTT samples in an episode. We see that for 90% of bufferbloat episodes the normalized additional delay is above one, which means the added delay due to buffering is more than the baseline RTT for the destinations of packets in the episode. In 70% of cases the additional delay is more than twice the baseline RTT. This result shows that when bufferbloat happens, it is a significant factor on end-to-end RTTs.

We also study by how much bufferbloat affects TCP connections, or how much longer TCP connections take to finish during bufferbloat episodes. Clearly, we cannot compare the same TCP connection during an episode and outside an episode. Instead, we study the median value of the duration of TCP connections in each environment and compare with the median duration during bufferbloat. Figure 6 presents the scatter plot of the median duration of TCP connections overall and during bufferbloat episodes per environment.

We see that the vast majority of points (90%) are above the x=y line. So on most environments bufferbloat increases the duration of TCP connections. In some environments, the median duration of TCP connections went from less than 100ms to over a few minutes. The impact of the longer duration will depend on the application, which we study next.

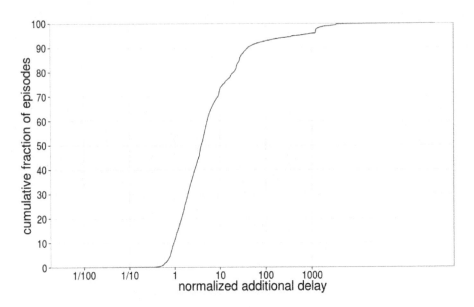

Fig. 5. Cumulative distribution of the median of the normalized additional delay during bufferbloat episodes. A normalized additional delay equal one means that the additional delay due to buffering is the same as the baseline RTT.

4.4 Bufferbloat Per Application

This section characterizes bufferbloat per application. Bloated delays are more severe for interactive applications than bulk, for instance. We want to understand which applications most often appear during bufferbloat episodes and by how much their RTTs increase during bufferbloat episodes. We divide the RTT samples in each episode according to the application executable name. Together the 55 users we monitor use hundreds of different applications. For simplicity of presentation, we manually group these applications into six classes: *streaming*, which includes applications such as real-player, VLC; *interactive*, e.g., Skype, SSH; *bulk*, with applications like Dropbox, P2P clients, FTP; *web*, with all browsers; *mail*, with Thunderbird, mail; *other*, which includes applications we couldn't fit in one of the previous categories. The HostView dataset has the application executable name for 84% of TCP connections. We exclude the 16% of connections for which we don't have an application name from the rest of the analysis in this section.

Table 1 presents the rank of application classes based on the percentage of the bufferbloat episodes with traffic from each application class. We see that the vast majority of episodes affected interactive and web applications. Both these applications are sensitive to additional delays of few hundreds of milliseconds. Although bulk applications are often pointed out as the cause of bufferbloat, not all bufferbloat episodes co-occurred with bulk applications. Note that we are only measuring one end-host behind the buffer, so it is possible that another

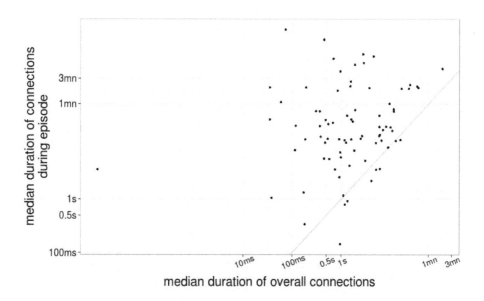

Fig. 6. Scatter plot of the median TCP connection duration per environment. Each point represents an environment. The x-axis is the median connection duration in the environment overall and the y-axis is the median connection duration only for connections that were affected by some bufferbloat episodes. The diagonal represents x=y.

Table 1. Percentage of bufferbloat episodes per application class

application class	% bufferbloat episodes
interactive	83.34%
web	80.40%
bulk	57.55%
other	41.97%
mail	38.99%
streaming	1.09%

end-host is doing a bulk transfer that is causing bufferbloat but we don't observe it in our data. Although we don't know which application is causing bufferbloat, we can say that all applications sending traffic during the episode will suffer from the additional delay.

We analyze the increase in TCP connections duration for interactive and web applications during bufferbloat episodes. Figure 7 replots the same metrics as in Figure 6 only for interactive and web traffic.

The duration of TCP connection for both web and interactive applications increase considerably during bufferbloat (the vast majority of points are above the x=y line). For example, our analysis of the data in this figure shows that in 75% of environments TCP connections of web last less than 12 seconds, but during

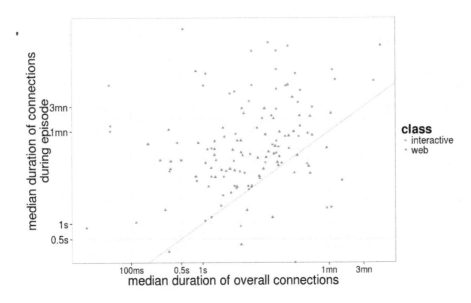

Fig. 7. Scatter plot of the median TCP connection duration for interactive and web applications per environment

bufferbloat only in a little over 36% of environments connections last less than 12 seconds. For interactive applications, in approximately 2% of environments TCP connections have a median duration above three minutes. This percentage increases to 40% during bufferbloat episodes.

Figure 8 presents the duration of bufferbloat episodes in seconds per application class. The distribution of episode duration is similar across application classes. The only small deviation is for bulk and streaming applications. The results for streaming may deviate simply because we don't have many streaming samples. Bufferbloat episodes that contain traffic of bulk applications that tend to last a bit longer when compared to other applications. This result is intuitive as bulk transfers tend to sustain a high transfer rate for longer periods of time.

5 Summary

This paper performed the first characterization of bufferbloat from data collected at end-hosts, where we can better gauge its impact on actual application performance as experienced by end-users. First, we designed an algorithm to detect buffering episodes from RTT samples passively collected at end-hosts. Our algorithm is robust to measurement noise and sparsity of RTT samples. It detects the beginning and end of each episode, which allow us to perform a more detailed characterization of buffering episodes. We define empirically that all buffering episodes that last for more than 200ms are bufferbloat episodes. Then, we apply this algorithm to data collected over Ethernet from 55 users

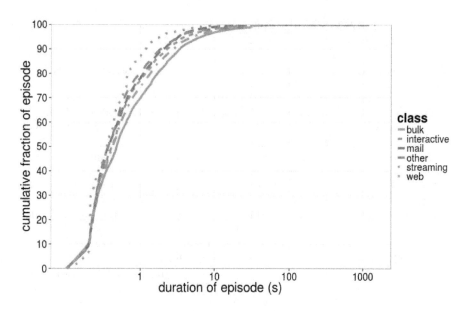

Fig. 8. Cumulative distribution of duration of bufferbloat episodes that affect each of the application classes

in 87 network environments to study bufferbloat in the wild. Our results show that most users do experience bufferbloat episodes that introduce from 200ms to over 22s of additional delay for a sustained period of time. The magnitude and duration of bufferbloat episodes depends heavily on the network environment. Furthermore, we find that during bufferbloat episodes RTTs are at least doubled and sometimes over one thousand times more than baseline latency for the same destinations. This additional delay impacts the duration of TCP connections. Our analysis per application shows that web and interactive applications, which are particularly sensitive to delays, are the most often affected by bufferbloat.

Acknowledgment. We thank Diana Joumblatt, Diego da Hora, and Oana Goga, for their contributions. We also thank shepherd, Philippe Owevarski. This work was partly done at the LINCS (Paris) and was supported by the European Commission's Seventh Framework Program (FP7/2007-2013) no. 258378 (FIGARO).

References

1. Kreibich, C., Weaver, N., Nechaev, B., Paxson, V.: Netalyzr: illuminating the edge network. In: Proceedings of the 10th ACM SIGCOMM Conference on Internet Measurement, IMC 2010, pp. 246–259. ACM, New York (2010), http://doi.acm.org/10.1145/1879141.1879173
2. Gettys, J., Nichols, K.: Bufferbloat: dark buffers in the internet. Commun. ACM 55(1), 57–65 (2012), http://doi.acm.org/10.1145/2063176.2063196

3. Nichols, K., Jacobson, V.: Controlling queue delay. Queue 10(5), 20:20–20:34 (2012), http://doi.acm.org/10.1145/2208917.2209336

4. Sundaresan, S., de Donato, W., Feamster, N., Teixeira, R., Crawford, S., Pescapè, A.: Broadband internet performance: A view from the gateway. SIGCOMM Comput. Commun. Rev. 41(4), 134–145 (2011), http://doi.acm.org/10.1145/2043164.2018452

5. DiCioccio, L., Teixeira, R., May, M., Kreibich, C.: Probe and pray: Using UPnP for home network measurements. In: Taft, N., Ricciato, F. (eds.) PAM 2012. LNCS, vol. 7192, pp. 96–105. Springer, Heidelberg (2012)

6. Chirichella, C., Rossi, D.: To the moon and back: are internet bufferbloat delays really that large? In: TMA (2013)

7. Allman, M.: Comments on bufferbloat. SIGCOMM Comput. Commun. Rev. 43(1), 30–37 (2012), http://doi.acm.org/10.1145/2427036.2427041

8. Ghobadi, M., Cheng, Y., Jain, A., Mathis, M.: Trickle: rate limiting youtube video streaming. In: Proceedings of the 2012 USENIX Conference on Annual Technical Conference, USENIX ATC 2012, p. 17. USENIX Association, Berkeley (2012), http://dl.acm.org/citation.cfm?id=2342821.2342838

9. Jiang, H., Wang, Y., Lee, K., Rhee, I.: Tackling bufferbloat in 3g/4g networks. In: Proceedings of the 2012 ACM Conference on Internet Measurement Conference, IMC 2012, pp. 329–342. ACM, New York (2012), http://doi.acm.org/10.1145/2398776.2398810

10. Joumblatt, D., Teixeira, R., Chandrashekar, J., Taft, N.: Hostview: annotating end-host performance measurements with user feedback. SIGMETRICS Perform. Eval. Rev. 38(3), 43–48 (2011), http://doi.acm.org/10.1145/1925019.1925028

11. Ostermann, S.: tcptrace, http://www.tcptrace.org/

12. Gringoli, F., Salgarelli, L., Dusi, M., Cascarano, N., Risso, F., Claffy, K.C.: Gt: picking up the truth from the ground for internet traffic. SIGCOMM Comput. Commun. Rev. 39(5), 12–18 (2009), http://doi.acm.org/10.1145/1629607.1629610

HoBBIT: A Platform for Monitoring Broadband Performance from the User Network

Walter de Donato, Alessio Botta, and Antonio Pescapé

University of Napoli Federico II, Italy
{walter.dedonato,a.botta,pescape}@unina.it

Abstract. In the last years the problem of measuring and monitoring broadband performance has attracted a lot of attention. In this paper we present our recent work in this area, providing the following main contributions: firstly, we analyze the literature, illustrating the different existing approaches and the main requirements of platforms implementing these approaches; secondly, we describe the lessons learned designing and implementing a platform called HoBBIT; thirdly, we analyze and share the results obtained from the current deployment in Italy. The lessons learned and the design guidelines of the platform can be of help in light of the recent research and standardization efforts in this area. The results and the dataset we shared with the community provide information on the current status of broadband in Italy and allow other researchers to access fresh measurements from a real and large scale deployment.

1 Introduction

Recently, a great interest has been focused on the performance evaluation of broadband access networks, in order to shed light on (i) what is the real experience perceived by users on a large scale [1] and (ii) to provide empirical data for policymakers [2]. Most projects pursuing this objective perform active measurements to evaluate common QoS metrics. They operate such measurements by adopting different techniques and from different viewpoints, each of them affecting obtained results in a different way: most projects require users to cooperate by running a software on their computer or by deploying a special device in their home network, acting as vantage points (VPs) to perform the measurements[1].

In this paper we describe our recent research work, basically providing a twofold contribution. On the one hand, (i) we briefly analyze the literature by providing a taxonomy of approaches for evaluating broadband performance; (ii) we identify the most effective ones by evaluating their pros and cons; (iii) we outline the main characteristics and requirements of a platform suitable for applying such approaches. On the other hand, (iv) we describe the solutions we adopted in designing and developing a measurement platform called HoBBIT[2]

---

[1] In this work we explicitly target fixed broadband access networks and related issues. Mobile broadband is out of the scope of this paper.

[2] http://hobbit.comics.unina.it

A. Dainotti, A. Mahanti, and S. Uhlig (Eds.): TMA 2014, LNCS 8406, pp. 65–77, 2014.

Fig. 1. A taxonomy for broadband performance evaluation approaches based on the location of the VPs initiating the measurements

(Host-Based Broadband Internet Telemetry); (v) we analyze the preliminary results obtained from the current deployment; (vi) we release open data sets to the community[3].

To highlight and summarize the significance of the contribution proposed in this work, we underline that, to the best of our knowledge, it extends the results in literature (a) by providing design guidelines for implementing platforms for large scale measurements of broadband accesses, and (b) by collecting, analyzing, and sharing a rich set of data from real users in a specific geographical region for 3 years. The importance of the contribution should also be seen in the light of the work that various bodies are doing for standardizing the different aspects related to these platforms (architectures[4], metrics[5], methodologies[6], use cases[7], etc.) and it is witnessed by recent events like the 1st NMRG workshop on large scale network measurements[8].

2   Platforms for Broadband Monitoring and Measurement

By analyzing the literature and the main projects addressing the evaluation of access network performance, we defined a simple but effective taxonomy. As illustrated in Fig. 1, it classifies the approaches depending on where the VPs initiating the measurements are located: *WAN-based* approaches exploit VPs deployed in Internet at different locations, such as the network of the user's *ISP* [3–5], *transit* networks [6,7], or *stub* networks hosting real services [8]; *UN-based* approaches deploy VPs inside the user's network, such as the home *gateway* [1,9] or a software running on generic *hosts* (laptops, tablets, etc.) in the form of a standalone *application* [10–15] or a *browser* executing a web application [16–18].

The study of the literature allowed to understand that all the approaches have both advantages and drawbacks, but those working from user network result to be more effective[9]: they can better take into account the context in which measurements are performed. Among them, we identify gateway- and application-based as

---

[3] http://traffic.comics.unina.it/Traces
[4] LMAP, https://datatracker.ietf.org/wg/lmap/charter/
[5] IPPM, https://datatracker.ietf.org/wg/ippm/charter/
[6] BMWG, https://datatracker.ietf.org/wg/bmwg/charter/
[7] HomeNet, https://datatracker.ietf.org/wg/homenet/charter/
[8] http://tinyurl.com/pqfkd7e
[9] We refer the reader to [19] for the details about such analysis.

the most promising approaches: they allow to perform repeated experiments on the same access link over a long time period, thus obtaining more statistically significant results. A trade-off exists between these two approaches: gateway-based ones are more accurate, but have some drawbacks (e.g., shipping devices is costly, gateways offer limited resources); client-based ones are less accurate (e.g., they cannot directly consider all the cross traffic potentially affecting measurement results), but enable to easily obtain capillary large-scale deployments. These aspects make the latter more effective for obtaining a fine-grained geographical view of broadband performance.

While in [9] we presented a gateway-based platform, in this work we describe what we learned while designing and implementing an application-based platform for measuring broadband access networks. We believe that this contribution can be of great help for the research and standardization efforts ongoing in this field and can stimulate fresh and interesting discussions at the workshop.

Proposed Reference Architecture. As illustrated in Fig. 2, a UN-based platform should include three essential components: (i) *measurement clients* (henceforth *clients*) running inside the user's network, which periodically ask for instructions about experiments to execute, and report back the obtained results; (ii) *measurement servers* (MRSs) acting as counterparts for active measurements, possibly deployed on networks with high-capacity links to the main backbones; (iii) a *management server*[10] (MGS) responsible for: configuring and planning experiments to be performed by clients; collecting, organizing, and storing measurement results; monitoring the operating state of clients and MRSs; pushing software updates to clients.

Platform Requirements. Ideally, VPs should cover all the geographic locations of interest, ISPs, and service plans (henceforth *plans*). MRSs should be properly distributed to have at least one of them at the shortest network distance, while their number should be proportional to the number of clients in a given location.

We further identify the following requirements:

- *scalability*: it should be able to cope with a large number of clients;
- *accuracy*: it should provide accurate measurements while avoiding significant interferences among them;
- *portability*: clients should be as portable as possible, in order to potentially involve any user;
- *flexibility*: performed measurements should be dynamically tunable to behave according to the context;
- *autonomicity*: it should automatically obtain any required information (e.g., plan details, geographical area) without relying on user cooperation (which may lead to unverifiable mistakes);
- *manageability*: it should provide an easy way to manage experiments (e.g., definition, configuration, deployment);
- *traceability*: every measurement taken should include a timestamp and refer to a well-identified access network;
- *non-intrusiveness*: it should mitigate the impact of measurements on user traffic;

---

[10] A single point of failure can be avoided by deploying multiple servers.

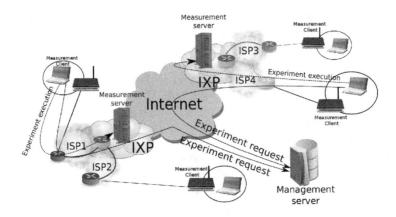

Fig. 2. Platform architecture overview

- *security*: it should not represent a potential vulnerability for the user network;
- *privacy*: collected data should always be treated in order to preserve user privacy;
- *(geolocalized) visibility*: collected data should be properly presented to the user as an incentive to participate;
- *independence*: it should operate independently on ISPs funding or control to guarantee unbiased results;
- *inexpensiveness*: the deployment cost should be limited in order to allow the number of clients to scale quickly.

3   The HoBBIT Platform

According to the guidelines defined in Sec. 2, we designed and implemented HoBBIT, an application-based platform currently operated on the Italian territory[11]. Volunteers can install a portable client application on their computer(s) for monitoring the performance of their access network(s).

Since HoBBIT clients can move among different access networks (henceforth *connections*), we designed the platform by using a connection-centric approach. Each connection is associated to its geographical position (up to the zip code granularity) and to its network details (i.e., *ISP*, *plan*). Every user may own more *installations* of the client, each possibly contributing to the performance evaluation of several connections. As for measurements, they are referred to as *experiments*, which are organized in *campaigns* having a specific goal. Each experiment is periodically executed following a detailed *schedule*, which is defined by the specific campaign. Each experiment can produce more than one *measurement output* (i.e., a set of samples collected at a specific sampling rate) or a *failure log*. Finally, a set of MRSs is available for supporting the experiments with part of their resources (*slices*).

At runtime – every 5 minutes – each client asks the MGS for a list of experiments. If the list is not empty, it sequentially executes all the experiments

---

[11] The deployment can be easily extended to other geographical areas.

and finally reports back all the results. All the messages exchanged between the clients and the MGS are XML-encoded and transferred over the HTTPS protocol. In the following, by adopting a problem/solution scheme, we briefly describe the main lessons we learned while designing and implementing HoBBIT, with the aim to satisfy most of the requirements outlined in Sec.2. We refer the reader to [19] for a detailed discussion.

Tracking Client-connection Associations. HoBBIT clients can move among different connections or operate together behind the same connection. This is primarily true for mobile devices (e.g., laptops, tablets), which are today really common. It is then necessary to properly track their association with connections, supporting also plan upgrades and ISP changes.

Solution. The client computes a hash value starting from the MAC address of its current default gateway, which is used by the MGS to uniquely identify the connection. The hash is computed adding to the string representing the MAC address a progressive number, which is incremented every time a plan upgrade or an ISP change is detected or notified by the user. Hence, the history of a connection can be reconstructed. Since a gateway may have more than one network interface (e.g., wired and wireless), different hash values may be associated to the same connection. To cope also with such case, we implement an aliasing condition: we consider two connections in alias only if different clients report the same public IP address close enough in time[12]. This solution enables different clients to be coordinated by the MGS for evaluating the performance of a connection. Hence, it helps to satisfy both accuracy and traceability requirements.

Detecting Service Plan and Location. Every time a new connection is identified, it is necessary to detect its main properties: ISP, plan details, and geographic location. We found that asking such information directly to users is not sufficient: they tend to leave the information empty or, worst, to provide wrong answers. This is particularly true for plan details (e.g., advertised downstream and upstream rates, and access technology), since most users do not have enough technical knowledge to provide correct information.

Solution. In order to mitigate as much as possible the voluntary or accidental introduction of errors caused by users, we adopted a semi-automatic approach that tries to obtain most of the information automatically, while requesting the remaining information to the user in a guided way. We automatically detect: i) the ISP, using the public IP address of the client; ii) the plan, matching the results of an ad-hoc measurement campaign against a database of existing ISPs and plans; iii) the location up to the zip code granularity (only if GPS is available). Then, we present the inferred information to the user on a web page, where he can confirm, correct, or refine it. This procedure is performed every time an unknown connection is detected and is aimed at providing autonomicity.

Providing a flexible measurement framework. In order to cope with heterogeneous and evolving network scenarios, the platform should be able to support any measurement tool and to dynamically adjust its parameters depending

---

[12] Since some ISPs assign to users private IP addresses, we apply the aliasing condition only if we detect one private hop between the client and the Internet.

on the context. Moreover, measurements should be scheduled according to the needs of the specific campaign, which may require to repeatedly execute an experiment at a specific time on a particular set of connections.

Solution. We designed the HoBBIT framework to give high flexibility in the definition, configuration and execution of the experiments and in their assignment to clients. On the one hand, each experiment is defined by the (P_i, P_o, S) tuple, where the P_i and P_o sets represent input and output parameters, and S is a wrapper script acting as an adaption layer between the client and the underlying measurement tool. On the other hand, each campaign can be assigned to a subset of connections by means of configurable parameters (e.g., all the DSL connections in a specific area).

Providing accurate measurements. Obtaining accurate results is fundamental for any measurement platform and, when focusing on the access network, it is important to isolate most of the confounding factors coming from both the user network and the Internet. Moreover, accurate tools should be adopted and their execution should be controlled in order to avoid excessive interferences. Indeed, since many clients conduct measurements toward a few servers, it is important to properly coordinate the execution of the experiments to avoid interferences on the server side.

Solution. In order to isolate most of the confounding factors, we adopt the following strategy: (i) we try to deploy dedicated MRSs in networks having high-capacity links to the main backbones (in order to push the bottleneck toward the access link) and in different locations (in order to be able to select the MRS closest to the client both in terms of end-to-end latency and hops); (ii) we avoid conducting measurements if user-generated traffic and CPU usage exceed thresholds defined for the connection (depending on upstream and downstream rates, access network capacity, etc.). (iii) since we cannot take into account all the interferences, we try to repeat as many measurements as possible in the same conditions (e.g., same daytime and day of week), in order to count on big numbers for isolating outliers; (iv) for each measurement, we take note of the involvement of a wireless link (e.g., Wi-Fi) between the host and the access link.

As for the accuracy of the tools, we purposely designed the measurement framework to support any underlying pre-existing tool. Hence, standard and well-tested tools are and can be adopted depending on the context.

To cope with server-side interferences, we designed a centralized scheduling algorithm executed by the MGS while assigning experiment targets to clients[13]. We assign MRSs a network capacity made of reservable fixed-size slices. For each slice we keep a timestamp representing the time when a slice will be free again. When a client asks for an experiment target MRS, the MGS reserves – according to the experiment duration and required bandwidth – the set of slices having the lower timestamp values on a single MRS. If not enough slices are immediately available, the reply includes a delay time, i.e. the time to wait before starting the experiment.

---

[13] Because of space constraints, we refer the reader to [19] for a detailed description of the algorithm.

Making the platform scalable. A platform conducting periodic measurements and potentially involving a huge number of clients has to properly address scalability from different viewpoints: i) network load introduced by both control and measurement traffic; ii) available computational and networking resources on MRSs; iii) storage and processing of the amount of data collected on the MGS(s).

Solution. While the scheduling algorithm described above allows to address the first two viewpoints by properly dimensioning the number of MRSs and tuning the periodicity of the experiments, further work is necessary to address the third one. Indeed, the amount of data collected over time tends to increase very quickly, and processing it in realtime becomes unfeasible without special arrangements. Since the objective is to maintain the finest granularity on the measurements performed (i.e. the samples produced by every single experiment) while offering different levels of aggregation on different axes (i.e. temporal and geographical), we structured the HoBBIT database in order to store and aggregate data in an efficient manner (e.g., materializing views, partitioning tables). To cope with the increasing amount of samples produced by every single experiment, we are also studying and comparing different reduction approaches.

Making the Platform Easily Manageable. To properly control and configure a complex platform made of several distributed nodes, it is fundamental to have a (logically) single management point, which should allow to easily reconfigure or update any part of the platform, in order to support remote troubleshooting and debugging without user intervention.

Solution. HoBBIT has been purposely designed to control any aspect of the platform from the MGS(s). It provides a web-based management interface which gives full control on the configuration of campaigns, experiments and related aspects, while giving visibility on monitored connections, installations running on them, and collected measurement results. Moreover, we can set any client in debug mode (to send detailed debug logs back to the MGS) and automatically update them in automatic or on-demand (i.e., only for specific clients) modes[14]. This solution provides manageability.

Involving as Many Users as Possible. The success of platforms like HoBBIT is determined by the ability to involve as many users as possible, possibly using different ISPs and plans, and with a large geographical coverage. Main problems here are the diversity of user equipments (PCs, OS, etc.) and the necessity to find effective incentives [20, 21].

Solution. In order to make the client portable to the most widespread operating systems, we made the following choices: i) we developed the client using the Qt libraries, which provide high portability and flexibility; ii) we selected the bash and gawk interpreters for implementing wrapper scripts, because they are natively available on Linux and Mac OSX, while they have Cygwin-based versions

---

[14] The HoBBIT client is not installed system wide and does not require administration privileges to perform updates.

Table 1. Experiments part of the BPE campaign

ID	Measured metrics	Adopted transport protocol	Required bandwidth (kbps)	Measure duration (sec)	Sampling rate (msec)
#1	Round-trip Latency, Jitter & Packet loss	UDP	0	30	1000
#2	Upstream throughput	UDP	$f(AR_{up})$	15	
#4		TCP			
#3	Downstream throughput	UDP	$f(AR_{dw})$		
#5		TCP			

for Windows[15]; iii) we select measurement tools according to their portability. As for providing incentives for the users, we give them visibility and guided interpretation on the performance measured, enabling the comparison with nearby connections.

Preserving User Experience. Frequent measurements are important to compensate the effect of confounding factors and to observe time-dependent trends. On the other side, it is fundamental to avoid a noticeable impact on user experience, to keep them involved in the long term.

Solution. The HoBBIT client has been purposely designed to provide nonintrusiveness. On the one hand, the user interface normally consists in a system tray icon displaying the current status (e.g., measure in progress, idle, etc.), while limited user interactions are required only when a new connection is detected. Moreover, interacting with the icon, the user can always know when the next set of experiments will be performed and decide to temporarily disable their execution for a predefined period (e.g., from half hour up to four hours). On the other hand, experiments are performed only if computational and networking resources are not over two different thresholds, defined according to the host capabilities and to the plan respectively. If after a number of retries such conditions are not satisfied, the experiment is aborted.

4   Experimental Analysis

Since December 2010 HoBBIT is running a measurement campaign named Basic Performance Evaluation (BPE). Its objective is to measure a basic set of performance metrics on a regular basis and for a long period. We present preliminary results from about 190K experiments performed on 310 selected connections monitored by the current deployment, which counts about 400 clients.

---

[15] Both the Cygwin library and the interpreters are embedded into the client.

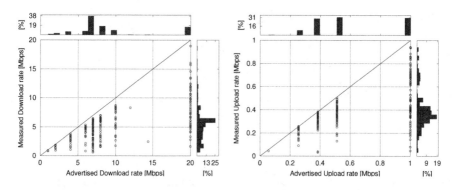

Fig. 3. Average discrepancy between advertised and actual performance

4.1 BPE Campaign Details

Tab. 1 reports details about BPE. Round-trip latency, jitter and packet loss are evaluated generating 10 isochronous UDP packets per second for 30 seconds, while upstream and downstream throughput are measured imposing for 15 seconds a constant bitrate – 5% higher than the advertised rate (AR) – with both UDP and TCP protocols. Such measurements are performed every half hour toward three MRSs located at the University of Napoli by embedding the D-ITG tool [22].

4.2 Preliminary Results from the Real Deployment

Analyzing the data collected, we tried to answer to the following important questions about broadband in Italy.

To What Extent ISPs Offer the Advertised Performance? Most ISPs advertise only the downstream and upstream capacity of their connections. We compared them with the average throughput results obtained for each monitored connection. Fig. 3 reports the comparison of measured and advertised rates in downstream (left) and upstream (right), where x and y axes respectively report advertised and measured speeds, each point identifies a monitored connection, and the histograms highlight their percentage with respect to both speeds. At first glance, it is evident how no connection meets or outperforms the advertised maximum rates. The discrepancy between actual and advertised performance is highly variable, ranging from 10% to 90% for downstream and from 5% to 100% for upstream. It is also noticeable that users owning high-end plans observe a higher performance penalty than those owning low-end plans. Clustering the observed ADSL performance by plans, some other characteristics are more evident. Fig. 4 – divided in four groups according to the advertised upstream capacity for ease of reading – reports the average rates measured in both directions, where each point (red 'o' marker) represents the measured rates of a connection and a line connects each of them to the corresponding advertised rates (black '*' marker). In this kind of plot nearly horizontal (vertical) lines

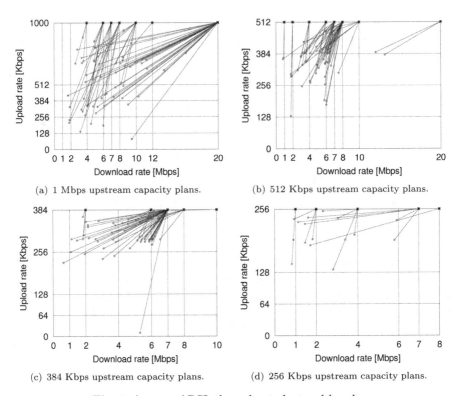

(a) 1 Mbps upstream capacity plans.

(b) 512 Kbps upstream capacity plans.

(c) 384 Kbps upstream capacity plans.

(d) 256 Kbps upstream capacity plans.

Fig. 4. Average ADSL throughput clustered by plan

highlight a very asymmetric discrepancy with respect to the downstream (up-stream) direction. On the one hand, Fig.4(a) highlights how 20 Mbps plans are in general very far from the promised maximum rates, which is a consequence of a technological constraint: the distance between the modem and the DSLAM is often too long to avoid excessive signal attenuation. Furthermore, 25% of moni-tored high-end plans (more expensive) achieve rates advertised by low-end plans (cheaper), causing a waste of money for the user. On the other hand, Fig.4(c) and 4(d) show how low advertised upstream rates are more likely to be achieved. From the above results, the answer is that actual performance unlikely reaches the maximum advertised rates and the difference between actual and measured rates is not negligible in many cases.

What Unadvertised QoS Metrics Do Different ISPs Provide.? By look-ing at unadvertised QoS parameters, different ISPs may offer significantly diverse performance. Fig. 5(b), 5(c), and 5(d) report the empirical cumulative distribu-tions of such metrics for four major Italian ISPs, for which HoBBIT monitored the amount of connections reported in Fig. 5(a). According to Fig. 5(b) all the ISPs provide latencies below 100 ms in 80% of cases, but only the Wind operator provides under 40 ms latencies in more than 50% of cases. On the other hand, according to Fig. 5(c) and Fig. 5(d), Wind provides high jitter values in more than 40% of cases and some packet losses in 25% of cases. A possible explanation

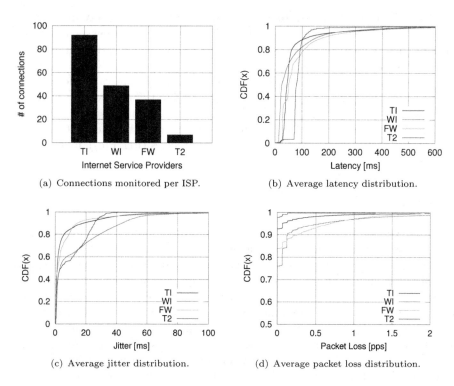

(a) Connections monitored per ISP.

(b) Average latency distribution.

(c) Average jitter distribution.

(d) Average packet loss distribution.

Fig. 5. Average unadvertised QoS metrics from 4 major Italian ISPs: Telecom Italia (TI), Wind (WI), Fastweb (FW), Tele2 (T2)

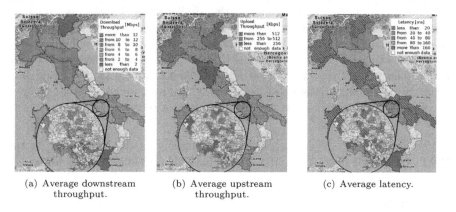

(a) Average downstream throughput.

(b) Average upstream throughput.

(c) Average latency.

Fig. 6. Average performance ranges measured: Italian regions and municipalities around Napoli

of such results is that Wind configures ADSL plans in fast mode, which provides low latencies at the cost of higher loss probability.

To What Extent Performance Depends on Geographic Location.? We analyzed the maps reported on the HoBBIT website. Fig. 6 shows average performance aggregated per region (nation wide) and per municipality (in the area around Napoli). While in average the downstream throughput (Fig. 6(a)) is between 4 and 6 Mbps in most regions, a few of them observe values lower than 2 Mbps and the same happens at municipality level. The average upstream throughput (Fig. 6(b)) is higher than 512 Kbps only in three regions and a few municipalities, while most of other areas provide values between 256 and 512 Kbps. Finally, only a few areas report average latencies (Fig. 6(c)) above 40 ms, both at region and municipality level.

5   Conclusion

Shedding light on broadband performance on a large scale is still a challenging task. In this work, starting from the definition of a taxonomy for the existing approaches, we presented the lessons we learned while designing and implementing HoBBIT, which tries to satisfy most of the requirements we identified as necessary to measure and monitor broadband performance from the user network, using an application-based approach. We discussed the main issues encountered and the practical solutions we adopted for them. Thanks to the deployment of HoBBIT on the Italian territory, we also collected and shared fresh results on the performance of broadband in Italy. By analyzing these measurements, we tried to answer three basic questions about the performance perceived by users. We detected that (i) in average most plans promise maximum rates which are far from actual average rates, (ii) 25% of HoBBIT users may obtain the same performance – and save money – by choosing a cheaper plan, and (iii) unadvertised QoS metrics can make the difference among similar plans. Finally, we underline that to obtain more reliable insights about performance on a geographic basis, a more capillary deployment is necessary. Accordingly, in our ongoing work we are investigating incentive mechanisms to reach a wider user participation. We further plan to perform an experimental comparison among HoBBIT and similar platforms, and to design and deploy in it new measurement techniques for detecting network neutrality violations and Internet censorship [23].

Acknowledgment. This work has been partially funded by MIUR in the PLATINO (PON01_01007) and SMART HEALTH (PON04a2_C) projects.

References

1. SamKnows, http://www.samknows.com/broadband/
2. Flamm, K., Friedlander, A., Horrigan, J., Lehr, W.: Measuring broadband: Improving communications policymaking through better data collection. Pew Internet & American Life Project (2007)
3. Cho, K., Fukuda, K., Esaki, H., Kato, A.: The impact and implications of the growth in residential user-to-user traffic. In: ACM SIGCOM (2006)

4. Siekkinen, M., Collange, D., Urvoy-Keller, G., Biersack, E.W.: Performance limitations of ADSL users: A case study. In: Uhlig, S., Papagiannaki, K., Bonaventure, O. (eds.) PAM 2007. LNCS, vol. 4427, pp. 145–154. Springer, Heidelberg (2007)
5. Maier, G., et al.: On dominant characteristics of residential broadband internet traffic. In: ACM Internet Measurement Conference (2009)
6. Dischinger, M., Haeberlen, A., Gummadi, K.P., Saroiu, S.: Characterizing residential broadband networks. In: Proc. ACM SIGCOMM Internet Measurement Conference, San Diego, CA, USA (October 2007)
7. Croce, D., En-Najjary, T., Urvoy-Keller, G., Biersack, E.: Capacity estimation of adsl links. In: CoNEXT (2008)
8. Youtube, http://www.youtube.com/my_speed
9. Sundaresan, S., de Donato, W., Feamster, N., Teixeira, R., Crawford, S., Pescapè, A.: Measuring home broadband performance. Communications of the ACM 55(11), 100–109 (2012)
10. Grenouille: Grenouille, http://www.grenouille.com/
11. Han, D., et al.: Mark-and-sweep: Getting the inside scoop on neighborhood networks. In: Proc. Internet Measurement Conference, Vouliagmeni, Greece (October 2008)
12. Bernardi, G., Marina, M.K.: Bsense: a system for enabling automated broadband census: short paper. In: Proc. of the 4th ACM Workshop on Networked Systems for Developing Regions, NSDR 2010 (2010)
13. Neubot, http://www.neubot.org
14. Ne.me.sys., https://www.misurainternet.it/nemesys.php
15. Joumblatt, D., et al.: Characterizing end-host application performance across multiple networking environments. In: 2012 Proceedings of IEEE INFOCOM, pp. 2536–2540. IEEE (2012)
16. Speedtest.net, http://www.speedtest.net
17. Kreibich, C., Weaver, N., Nechaev, B., Paxson, V.: Netalyzr: Illuminating the edge network. In: Proc. Internet Measurement Conference, Melbourne, Australia (November 2010)
18. Glasnost: Bringing Transparency to the Internet, http://broadband.mpi-sws.mpg.de/transparency
19. de Donato, W.: Large scale benchmarking of broadband access networks: Issues, methodologies, and solutions. PhD dissertation, University of Napoli Federico II (2011)
20. Lee, J.-S., Hoh, B.: Dynamic pricing incentive for participatory sensing. Pervasive and Mobile Computing 6(6) (2010)
21. Choffnes, D.R., Bustamante, F.E., Ge, Z.: Crowdsourcing service-level network event monitoring. ACM SIGCOMM Computer Communication Review 40(4), 387–398 (2010)
22. Botta, A., Dainotti, A., Pescapé, A.: A tool for the generation of realistic network workload for emerging networking scenarios. Computer Networks 56(15), 3531–3547 (2012)
23. Aceto, G., et al.: User-side approach for censorship detection: home-router and client-based platforms, Connaught Summer Institute on Monitoring Internet Openness and Rights, University of Toronto (2013)

Predictive Estimation of Wireless Link Performance from Medium Physical Parameters Using Support Vector Regression and k-Nearest Neighbors

Guillaume Kremer[1,2], Philippe Owezarski[1,2],
Pascal Berthou[1,2], and German Capdehourat[3]

[1] CNRS, LAAS, 7 avenue du colonel Roche, 31400 Toulouse, France
[2] Univ. de Toulouse, UPS, INSA, LAAS, 31400 Toulouse, France
[3] Instituto de Ingeniería Eléctrica, Facultad de Ingeniería,
Universidad de la República, Uruguay
{kremer,owe,berthou}@laas.fr, gcapde@fing.edu.uy

Abstract. In wireless networks, the physical medium is the cause of most of the errors and performance drops. Thus, an efficient predictive estimation of wireless networks performance w.r.t. medium status by the communication peers would be a leap ahead in the improvement of wireless communication. For that purpose, we designed a measurement bench that allows us to accurately control the noise level on an unidirectional WIFI communication link in the protected environment of an anechoic room. This way, we generated different medium conditions and collected several measurements for various PHY layer parameters on that link. Using the collected data, we analyzed the ability to predictively estimate the throughput performance of a noisy wireless link from measured physical medium parameters, using machine learning (ML) algorithms. For this purpose, we chose two different classes of ML algorithms, namely SVR (Support Vector Regression) [1] and k-NN (k-Nearest Neighbors) [2], to study the tradeoff between complexity and estimation accuracy. Finally, we ranked the pertinence of the most common physical parameters for estimating or predicting the throughput that can be expected by users on top of the IP layer over a WIFI link.

1 Introduction

Wireless networks are of essential importance nowadays. Users are more and more mobile and access the Internet thanks to mobile devices as laptops, smart phones or tablets. Even when staying at home, users want to get rid of wires. However, the wireless medium does not provide the same capabilities as wired networks on copper or fiber. In wireless networks, the physical medium is limited in terms of capacity, and the cause of most of the errors and performance drops. From a user or administrator point of view, the quality of wireless communication can appear as very versatile and unpredictable. This makes wireless

A. Dainotti, A. Mahanti, and S. Uhlig (Eds.): TMA 2014, LNCS 8406, pp. 78–90, 2014.

networks very complex to manage, and users often experience communication quality drops that are completely unexpected.

Monitoring wireless networks is then very difficult. Monitoring such networks at the IP layer is very inefficient (whereas it is the way it is done in wired networks with extremely good results). Some previous work tried to include the MAC level in the monitoring of wireless networks [3], but none integrates the full monitoring of the network from physical to network layers. We nevertheless argue that this is the direction to follow, and propose our preliminary study to estimate the relations between the physical signal parameters and the performance at the network level. Physicists are doing very strong studies on the signal level, but do not study the impact on upper layers [4]. In this paper, it is proposed to bridge the gap between the signal and the digital world in wireless communication networks.

This paper then presents a double contribution.

First, we designed and built a platform for benchmarking wireless communications. Many wireless testbeds, identified in the literature, already exist for that purpose. However, the major trend is to build large grid of wireless nodes which can be programmed individually to transmit, receive and/or measure data. Custom topologies can be made out of the grid by switching on and off nodes. For example, Orbits [5] follows this approach. However, these platforms are built in open environments and lack the isolation and environmental control required to conduct an accurate cross-layer study on wireless networks. Contrary to these works, our testbed is built in an anechoic chamber to fully control the experimental environment, and avoid external signals to disturb the behavior of the communicating devices and the quality of the measurements. We used on this platform the common digital communications devices that are widely used (laptops, tablets, smart phones), as well as dedicated signal measurement tools specifically designed for physicists. Anyway, because of space limit, this paper concentrates on the study of a WIFI link.

Second, the paper presents the analysis of the relations between the PHY parameters of the WIFI connection, and the performance parameters on top of the IP layer. It aims at demonstrating that, at the opposite of wired networks, the monitoring of wireless network can not avoid monitoring the physical level. It is shown that using a very limited number of signal parameters (one or two), it is possible to very accurately estimate communication performance and quality parameters as network level throughput, delay or loss ratio. With a carefully selected and set ML algorithm, it is even possible to predict performance drops at the scale of one second. For this purpose we rely on two kinds of supervised ML algorithms: SVR and k-NN. Both of them are known to have good prediction capabilities and to succeed in many domains as long as these domains can provide accurate time series [2, 6]. However their operational characteristics are very different making them more prone to different usage and applications. For example, SVR algorithms are strong learners whereas k-NN's learning is weak, thus making them unable to assimilate training data on the fly because of the huge computational complexity. However, SVR algorithms are more sophisticated than k-NN and so are more efficient to generalize data and usually more accurate on the estimations [2]. Therefore, we will compare the relative estimation performances obtained with SVR and k-NN as well as their performance concerning their time of execution (learning and estimation delays). Again, because of space limit, the paper only presents the results with the most common physical signal parameters as SNR or RSS for estimating the throughput obtained on top of the IP layer.

2   Machine Learning Algorithms

2.1   SVR Theory

This section presents the basic theory behind SVR. More details can be found in [7]. Given a set of training data $\{(x_1, y_1), ..., (x_n, y_n)\} \in \mathbb{X} \times \mathbb{R}$ with $\mathbb{X}$ the input space. The purpose of SVR algorithm is to estimate a function $f(x)$ with the requirements of having at most ϵ deviations from the targets y_i. Equations (1) and (2) show respectively SVR approximation for linear and non-linear form, with $\langle .,. \rangle$ the notation for the dot product in $\mathbb{X}$. In the linear case, SVR performs a linear regression in the input space. In the non-linear case, no regression can be done in the input space. Therefore, on a first hand, the SVR algorithm has to map the data into some feature space $\mathbb{F}$ via the function $\phi : \mathbb{X} \to \mathbb{F}$. On a second hand, the classical SV regression algorithm is applied in the new feature space.

$$f(x) = \langle w, x \rangle + b \text{ with } w \in \mathbb{X} \text{ and } b \in \mathbb{R}. \tag{1}$$
$$f(x) = \langle w, \phi(x) \rangle + b \text{ with } w \in \mathbb{X} \text{ and } b \in \mathbb{R}. \tag{2}$$

The second requirement for the regression is to maximize the "flatness" of the weights, here measured by $\|w\|^2$. Hence, in the non-linear case both coefficients w and b are estimated by minimizing the regularized risk function given in (4). In this equation, C is a user-defined constant which controls the trade-off between the training error and the model flatness. L_ϵ is the ϵ-insensitive loss function defined by equation (3). This function allows the SVR algorithm to only penalize estimation errors greater than ϵ.

$$L_\epsilon(y_i, f(x(i), w)) = \begin{cases} |y_i - f(x(i), w)| - \epsilon & \text{if } |y_i - f(x(i), w)| \geq \epsilon. \\ 0 & \text{otherwise.} \end{cases} \tag{3}$$

$$R(f, C) = C \sum_{i=1}^{n} L_\epsilon(y_i, f(x(i), w)) + \frac{1}{2} \|w\|^2. \tag{4}$$

To complete the regression we need to solve a convex optimization problem, which is more easily done by maximizing its dual form and introducing the Lagrange multipliers (α_i, α_j^*). The new optimization problem is given by (5) and is subject to $\sum_{i=1}^{n} (\alpha_i - \alpha_i^*) = 0$ and $\alpha_i^* \in [0, C]$.

$$\text{Maximize } -\frac{1}{2} \sum_{i,j=1}^{n} (\alpha_i - \alpha_i^*)(\alpha_j - \alpha_j^*)\langle \phi(x_i, x_j) \rangle \\ -\epsilon \sum_{i=1}^{n} (\alpha_i + \alpha_i^*) + \sum_{i=1}^{n} y(i)(\alpha_i - \alpha_i*). \tag{5}$$

Solving this leads to a new definition of (2) as $f(x) = \sum_{i=1}^{n}(\alpha_i - \alpha_i^*)\langle \phi(x_i), \phi(x)\rangle + b$.

At this point, this definition shows that the solution can be found by only knowing $\langle \phi(x_i), \phi(x)\rangle$ instead of explicitly knowing ϕ. A function $k(x, x')$ which corresponds to a dot product in some feature space $\mathbb{F}$ as defined by $k(x, x') = \langle \phi(x), \phi(x')\rangle$ is called a kernel. This kernel function can be any symmetric function satisfying Mercer condition such as the Gaussian Radial Basis (RBF) which is defined by $K(x_i, x_j) = \exp(-\gamma \|x_i - x_j\|^2)$. The Gaussian kernel is parametrized by γ ($\gamma > 0$) which impacts the generalization capability of the regressor among other things.

2.2 k-NN for Continuous Variables Estimation Theory

The learning approach of k-NN [8] is to memorize the entire training set. As so, the algorithm belongs to the class of the so-called lazy learners as [9, 10] for instance. Given a set of training data $D = \{(x_1, y_1), ..., (x_n, y_n)\} \in \mathbb{X} \times \mathbb{R}$, with $\mathbb{X} \subseteq \mathbb{R}$, the process followed by k-NN to estimate an object $z = (x', y')$ can be easily summed-up in three steps. Firstly, the algorithm computes the distance $d(x', x)$ between z and every object $(x_i, y_i) \in D$. Secondly, the set F of the k closest neighbors to z is selected. Thirdly, k-NN computes the estimation as $\hat{y} = \frac{1}{k}\sum_{i=1}^{k} x_i$ with $x \in F$. Variants exist and concern essentially the method used to compute the distance $d(x, x')$ such as the Manhattan, Euclidean or Minkowski distance. The p-order Minkowski distance for two sets of points $F = (x_1, ...x_n)$ and $G = (y_1, ..., y_n) \in \mathbb{R}^n$ is defined by $(\sum_{i=1}^{n} |x_i - y_i|)^{\frac{1}{p}}$.

3 Experimental Platform and Dataset

3.1 Experimental Conditions and Measurement Equipments

The implementation of a dedicated wireless testbed is a major requirement for our work. First of all, experimentations must be reproducible, allowing comparison between different sets of measurements and algorithms. This point is not trivial when using wireless networks as the environment factors have a high impact on the network performances. Secondly, part of the originality of this work comes from the combination of measurements made at multiple network layers, using electronics instruments and software tools. This was also a strong requirement to be able to monitor the physical layer (the wireless transmission), and compare it to the higher layers, from the mac layer information given by the network cards to the end-to-end layers as transport throughput for instance. The hardware introspection requirement has an impact on the components choice as explained below. Thirdly, the synchronization of all of these datasets was a sticky point, but absolutely required to ensure a good behavior of the learning algorithms.

3.2   Reproducibility Requirement

Our wireless testbed was designed inside an anechoic room. An anechoic room is a protected RF room which simulates free space conditions. Our model of chamber is 4,10 meters long for 2,50 meters wide. Inside, walls are covered of microwave absorbers materials that break and scatter any wireless signal that would come from an inside source. The chamber is then free of any multi-path propagation. There are different types of absorbers, each of them is defined for a specific frequency range that allows us to use the anechoic chamber for different purposes and frequencies. The absorbers protect also the inner environment of the room from outside perturbations. This protected context minimizes the uncontrolled parameters of our communication.

3.3   Introspection Requirement and Components Choice

Inside the anechoic chamber we placed two WIFI nodes. The nodes are controlled through a wired network to avoid interference with the wireless communication. The nodes are Avila-GW2348-4 gateway platforms and run a Linux OpenWrt OS. The boxes have an Intel Xscale processor, 64 MB of SDRAM and 16MBytes of Flash memory. The WIFI network controllers are based on the AR5414 chipset from Atheros which uses the ath5k driver and are attached to an omnidirectional antenna. The choice of the wifi chipset and its driver was crucial because they define the amount of metrics and the accuracy that it will be possible to obtain. The ath5k driver is open-source and well documented thanks to an active online community support. It has also a good integration within the OpenWrt OS. The OpenWrt OS is flexible enough to allow the implementation of new functionalities so that it accelerates the upgrade of the bench. In addition and because we were unable to capture the noise strength of the received signal with the Atheros hardware, we used an oscilloscope connected to the receiver antenna. It records the amplitude of the received signal. The oscilloscope chosen was a fast Lecroy WaveRunner which allows us to capture a maximum number of frame signal with little loss and to record them on internal memory. The precision of this instrument gives us the ground truth required by the training methods used. It also embeds a large library of filters, and operators which can be applied on the input signals. The oscilloscope is also synchronized by NTP.

Synchronization Requirement. As we used several equipments to get measurements, it is needed to have their clock very accurately synchronized. This was done with NTP by using a dedicated wired connection to a remote NTP server (accuracy with a shared network bus is not sufficient).

Capture and Measurement Processes. The configuration of the network interfaces is done in promiscuous mode to capture any packets sensed by their antenna. The packets are captured at the MAC layer using the PCAP library and tools when they arrive at the kernel interface. The packets contain data from link to application layers, such as the 802.11 channel number, the type of frame at the MAC layer, or packet size at the network layer. Additionally, a packet also contains a RADIOTAP header which gives radio level information such as the received signal strength (RSS) reported by the ath5k driver. We modified the ath5k drivers of the OpenWrt OS to permit, when possible, the propagation of packets with frame check sequence (FCS) errors to the upper layers, while on the original kernel they were discarded. The propagation is only possible if the error corrupted the data but not the header fields. Following this modification the RADIOTAP header now contains a flag specifying whether a FCS error was detected when decoding the packet.

The Lecroy oscilloscope was set to capture and flush the data as soon as a frame is detected on the input cable. This happens when the amplitude of the sensed signal is above a specific threshold, set to be in between the current noise floor and the minimal amplitude value of a frame. This threshold has to be set in a way to prevent exceptional high noise values that could be incorrectly detected as a frame.

3.4   Experimental Protocol

Noise Generation. One of the objectives of our environment is to minimize the presence of these uncontrolled parameters on the communication. Another objective is to generate and control selected parameters that will impact our communications.

The noise and the interferences significantly impact the communication. We then inject noise in the environment using a signal generator to perturb the communication. The signal generator is a device which emits RF signals. It can be configured to generate very realistic noise. Among the parameters of the generated noise, two important elements have a crucial impact: on a first hand the modulation used characterizes the main characteristics of the noise signal in the time and frequency domains (i.e. it characterizes the spectral occupancy of the generated signal, its fading or narrowness). On a second hand, the amplitude of the signal also affects the measured level of noise on the receiver side. We found that the AWGN (Adaptive White Gaussian Noise) noise modulation was a good choice for our preliminary studies because of its simplicity. Moreover it can be used to impact the entire bandwidth of a 802.11g channel contrary to most other modulation schemes which produce narrow band noise. The noise level was determined empirically by testing the effects on the communication. Finally, a major element that affects the noise generated in the anechoic chamber is the antenna. It characterizes the waveform, the direction and the amplitude of the noise wave. In order to perturb only one side of the communication we used a very directional antenna pointed to the receiving station. We use IPERF to generate traffic between the two peers. The traffic is a TCP flow with a constant throughput of 24 Mb/s. The size of the packets is set to 1470 bytes.

Training and Datasets. We generated different samples with different noise levels and different transmission powers. All the samples have the same duration of 5 minutes and will be used to constitute our training datasets. Table 1 sums

Table 1. Constitutions and characteristics of our training sets. Each vector represents 1 second of measurements.

Training set	Dataset definition
notation	{Tx Power (dBm); Noise Power (dBm)}; {sample 2};...
Dataset1 (5323 vectors)	{10;-20};{10;-17};{10;-15};{10;-13};{10;-10};{10;-7};{10;-5}; {20;-20};{20;-17};{20;-15};{20;-13};{20;-10};{20;-7};{20;-5}
Dataset2 (2661 vectors)	{10;-20};{10;-17};{10;-15};{10;-13};{20;-20};{20;-17};{20;-15};{20;-13}
Dataset3 (1330 vectors)	{10;-20};{10;-17};{10;-15};{10;-7};{10;-5};{20;-20};

up the characteristics of the different samples. The same experimental settings (transmission power and noise) are used for training and testing. Therefore a training dataset which contains all these samples will be considered as having full knowledge about the possible use cases met in the test dataset. Hence, to test the generalization capacity of our algorithm, we built three different training datasets as described in table 1. These datasets differ by the quantities of samples they are made of, and consequently by the level of knowledge they represent.

3.5 SVR Features Definitions

Atheros Received Throughput. This is the performance metric of the communication that we are considering in this paper. It is computed from the PCAP captured at the receiver side of the transmission. It is defined by $BW_i = \sum_{k=1}^{n} L(p_k)$ with $k \in \mathbb{N}$. BW_i is the computed throughput at second i, $L(p_k)$ is the length of the payload at the network layer for packet p_k such as $p_k \in P_i$ which is defined as the set of the nth received packets without FCS error during second i: $P_i = \{p_1, ..., p_n\}$.

Atheros RSS. The Atheros RSS is extracted from the RSS field in the RADIOTAP headers of the packets included in the PCAP files. Given that $RSS(p_k)$ is the RSS of packet p_k such as $p_k \in P_i$, and R_i is the set of RSS extracted from packets captured during second i, it is defined as $ATH\_RSS_i = \overline{R_i}$ with $R_i = \{RSS(p_1), ..., RSS(p_n))\}$.

Lecroy Noise. In addition to the Atheros values, we extract different metrics from the Lecroy datasets. These values are computed from the Root Mean Square (RMS) values of the raw data. These RMS values can be split into three parts, which are the data that are before, during and after the frame. The part of the data before and after the frame are the noise values and therefore can be used to extract the noise floor during the reception of that frame. We consider A and C, the sets of these points. Therefore we compute the average noise floor of the data during the reception of frame f with $N_f = \overline{A \cup C}$.

With M_i the set of noise levels extracted from the frames captured by the Lecroy oscilloscope during second i, we compute the feature for the noise floor at second i $LECR\_NOISE_i$ as $LECR\_NOISE_i = \overline{M_i}$ with $M_i = \{N_{p_1}, ..., N_{p_n}\}$ and $p_k \in P_i$.

Lecroy RSS. The RSS of the received frame is computed on the first 8 symbols to comply with 802.11 standard (see *http://standards.ieee.org/getieee802/*). These points constitute the set D. Thus, similarly to previous equations, the RSS for a frame f is given by $R_f = \overline{D}$ and $LECR\_RSS_i = \{R_{p_1}, ..., R_{p_n}\}$, where $LECR\_RSS_i$ is the feature of the Lecroy RSS at second i.

Lecroy SNR. Finally we compute the SNR S_f for frame f as the difference between the noise floor and the RSS of the frame P and therefore, similarly to previous formulas: $S_f = R_f - N_f$ and $LECR\_SNR_i = \overline{W_i}$ with $W_i = \{S_{p_1}, ..., S_{p_n}\}$ and $p_k \in P_i$.

4 Estimation of the Relations between Physical and Performance Parameters in WIFI Communications

4.1 ML Based Methodology

The 2nd contribution of this paper is the analysis of the relations linking the PHY layer parameters and the upper layers performance.

SVR. SVR algorithm has been used with RBF as a kernel function. As section 2.1 points it out, in our configuration SVR requires three user-defined parameters (C, γ and ϵ) which can impact performance and therefore must be carefully selected with regard to the application. For our estimations, we used a grid search to select these SVR parameters. It is a common empirical method which consists in an exhaustive test run of SVR training using generated settings combinations. We then select the best combination of C, γ and ϵ among the results.

k-NN. For the performance of k-NN, the value of k must be carefully selected. Therefore, after several tests on the different datasets, we chose a value which allows a good tradeoff between the estimation accuracy and the generalization results. Hence, in the presented experimentation, we set the value of k to 3. The distance method used is Minkowski with order 2 which corresponds to the Euclidean distance recommended with the traditional version of the algorithm [8].

Training and Estimation Delays Measurements. One part of the analysis of the machine learning estimations concerns the computational time associated with the training and estimations process. Our ML setup uses Python scikit-learn implementation [11] of SVR and k-NN. The delays are computed by reading the current clock using the 'time' function. The clock is read twice: before and after the measured process. The difference of the two measures constitutes the delay for the measured process. For each estimation, we made 100 runs and then computed the average and standard deviation of the delays. The CPU used to conduct the measures is a 64 bits Intel Core 2 Duo (2x2.53 GHz) with 6 MB of cache memory. The computer disposes of 4 GB of RAM memory. The operating system is Debian Linux.

4.2   Estimation Performance

To evaluate the estimations, two methods are used.

Mean Squared Error (MSE). Given that $\hat{Y}_i, ..., \hat{Y}_n$ are estimations and $Y_i, ..., Y_n$ are the real values, the MSE is defined as $MSE = \frac{1}{n} \sum_{i=1}^{n} (\hat{Y}_i - Y_i)^2$.

Percentage of Correct Estimations. We also use the percentage of correct estimations noted $P(e < d)$ and defined by $P(e < d) = \frac{1}{n} \sum_{i=1}^{n} D(\hat{Y}_i, Y_i, d)$. This value is the percentage of estimations which differ from the corresponding real values by less than a defined threshold d as shown on equation (6). These estimations are then considered 'correct'. Given the maximum throughput of 24 Mbps and the size of the packets defined to be 1470 bytes, we set the value of the threshold d to 1 Mbps. Indeed, this threshold corresponds to an error in the estimation of 4% (89 packets over 2139 transmitted during one second). By considering the preliminary measured performance of the algorithms this value could be considered to be fair to assess the goodness of the algorithms.

$$D(\hat{Y}_i, Y_i, d) = \begin{cases} 1 & \text{if } |\hat{Y}_i - Y_i| < d. \\ 0 & \text{if } |\hat{Y}_i - Y_i| \geq d. \end{cases} \tag{6}$$

4.3   Estimation Results

Table 2(a) contains the results of the throughput estimation based on 6 different PHY or combinations of PHY parameters for respectively Dataset1, Dataset2, and Dataset3. The first column quotes the PHY parameters that have been used for the SVR estimation of the IP throughput. The figures are obtained for the MSE and the probability P(e < 1Mb) for both ML algorithms. Table 2(b) gives the ranking for the PHY parameters according to their ability to allow good estimations of the throughput. A ranking of 1 corresponds to the best result among the 6 PHY parameters considered.

For *Dataset1*, i.e. the full one, the best result is obtained with *LECR_RSS + LECR_NOISE* for both families of algorithms. The estimations for SVR are plotted on figure 1. This figure exhibits impressive matching between the real and estimated values of the throughput, with just very few outliers appearing (75% matchings). We got as impressive results for *Dataset2*, and *Dataset3*, but this time, the best results for SVR have been obtained with the *LECR_SNR*

Table 2. Results of the estimations using physical layer metrics. $D1$, $D2$ and $D3$ stands respectively for $Dataset1$, $Dataset2$ and $Dataset3$.

(a) Scores of the estimations.

Physical layer parameter(s)		MSE (Mbps^2)								P(e < 1Mbps) (%)					
		SVR			k-NN			SVR			k-NN				
n°		D1	D2	D3	D1	D2	D3	D1	D2	D3	D1	D2	D3		
1	ATH_RSS	11.24	11	10.17	23	33	34	35	33	34	24	22	14		
2	$LECR\_RSS$	4.42	3.9	4.5	27	7.1	10	51	59	32	18	35	31		
3	$LECR\_NOISE$	2.28	5.4	5.8	5	2.8	4.2	69	55	44	50	44	24		
4	$LECR\_SNR$	1.69	**1.6**	**1.6**	4	2.3	2.8	64	**66**	**62**	48	50	45		
5	$ATH\_RSS + LECR\_NOISE$	1.02	2.3	3.3	4	1.3	**1.7**	70	49	41	54	60	**50**		
6	$LECR\_RSS + LECR\_NOISE$	**0.88**	2.0	2.53	**2**	**1.2**	2.2	**75**	57	49	**64**	**63**	46		

(b) Pertinence of the estimations.

Physical layer parameter(s)		SVR Pertinence ranking						k-NN Pertinence ranking					
		MSE			P(e < 1Mbps)			MSE			P(e < 1Mbps)		
n°		D1	D2	D3	D1	D2	D3	D1	D2	D3	D1	D2	D3
1	ATH_RSS	6	6	6	6	6	5	6	6	6	5	6	6
2	$LECR\_RSS$	5	4	4	5	2	6	5	5	5	6	5	4
3	$LECR\_NOISE$	4	5	5	3	4	3	4	4	4	3	4	5
4	$LECR\_SNR$	3	1	1	4	1	1	2	3	3	4	3	3
5	$ATH\_RSS + LECR\_NOISE$	2	3	3	2	5	4	2	2	1	2	2	1
6	$LECR\_RSS + LECR\_NOISE$	1	2	2	1	3	2	1	1	2	1	1	2

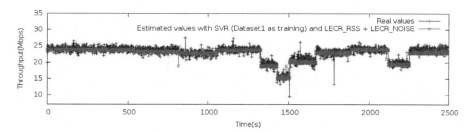

Fig. 1. Throughput estimation results obtained with the $LECR\_RSS + LECR\_NOISE$ metric compared to the real throughput

parameter (60% matchings). The difference of the results when using a full trace for the training compared to a sampled one exhibits the non empty intersection between PHY parameters as SNR, RSS and NOISE. These 3 parameters are closely related. The results for k-NN improve with the use of $Dataset2$. Contrary to SVR, the best estimations are obtained with the features 5 and 6 for every training datasets. Generally speaking, SVR performs better than k-NN excepts in the 2nd training dataset where k-NN outperforms SVR in terms of MSE. It nevertheless clearly appears with these figures that SNR, RSS and NOISE can help to perfectly estimate and predict (on a one second scale) the performance of the network at layers 3 and 4. Nevertheless, a deeper analysis on larger datasets, that still need to be produced, would allow a more accurate characterization of the link between PHY parameters and network performance. Actually, it appears that while the combined features metrics performance decreases, the overall performance of the RSS metrics 1 and 2 increases or stays more or less the same. This seems to suggest that the full training set was not adapted to these metrics. This is even more visible in k-NN results, while MSE performances improve impressively between *Dataset1* and *Dataset2*.

The difference between the full and the reduced sets is that the samples obtained with high noise are not present in the reduced datasets. This could be caused by incoherent values existing in *Dataset1* because of the bad and noisy conditions. One possibility is that these values could deteriorate the model issued from the training process. This hypothesis seems to be corroborated by the results obtained with k-NN and the simplicity of its algorithm which makes it more sensible to the general quality of the training dataset and the choice of the feature. This aspect needs to be considered for improving our platform and experiment protocol.

Table 3. Results of the measured delays for training and estimations using physical layer metrics. $D1$, $D2$ and $D3$ stands respectively for *Dataset1*, *Dataset2* and *Dataset3*.

(a) Average delays observed for the training processes on 100 runs (values into brackets are the standard deviation of the distributions. Due to space limitation, standard deviation values are given in 10^3 unit).

Physical layer parameter(s)	Time used for training (s)					
	SVR			k-NN		
$n°$	D1	D2	D3	D1	D2	D3
1 *ATH_RSS*	5.39 *(40)*	1.40 *(2)*	0.36 *(0.4)*	0.048 *(2)*	**0.023** *(0.1)*	**0.012** *(0.1)*
2 *LECR_RSS*	41.27 *(300)*	11.71 *(7)*	3.12 *(2)*	0.048 *(1)*	**0.023** *(0.2)*	**0.012** *(0.1)*
3 *LECR_NOISE*	5.17 *(10)*	1.38 *(1)*	0.36 *(0.8)*	0.051 *(6)*	**0.023** *(0.2)*	**0.012** *(0.1)*
4 *LECR_SNR*	11.54 *(6)*	3.87 *(4)*	1.35 *(2)*	0.048 *(4)*	**0.023** *(0.2)*	**0.012** *(0.1)*
5 *ATH_RSS + LECR_NOISE*	**4.50** *(4)*	**1.15** *(2)*	0.30 *(0.2)*	0.048 *(0.6)*	**0.023** *(0.1)*	**0.012** *(0.1)*
6 *LECR_RSS + LECR_NOISE*	4.72 *(9)*	1.23 *(2)*	**0.31** *(3)*	**0.046** *(0.5)*	**0.023** *(0.1)*	**0.012** *(0.08)*

(b) Average delays observed for the estimations processes on 100 runs (values into brackets are the standard deviation of the distributions. Due to space limitation, standard deviation values are given in 10^3 unit).

Physical layer parameter(s)	Time used for estimation (s)					
	SVR			k-NN		
$n°$	D1	D2	D3	D1	D2	D3
1 *ATH_RSS*	1.52 *(10)*	0.78 *(6)*	0.40 *(3)*	1.13 *(10)*	0.63 *(1)*	0.39 *(0.6)*
2 *LECR_RSS*	1.58 *(20)*	0.81 *(10)*	0.42 *(3)*	0.61 *(3)*	0.44 *(0.8)*	0.29 *(0.6)*
3 *LECR_NOISE*	1.47 *(20)*	0.76 *(10)*	0.42 *(4)*	0.96 *(30)*	0.35 *(0.9)*	0.08 *(0.3)*
4 *LECR_SNR*	1.38 *(30)*	0.70 *(10)*	0.36 *(3)*	0.74 *(60)*	0.45 *(0.8)*	0.19 *(0.3)*
5 *ATH_RSS + LECR_NOISE*	**1.34** *(9)*	**0.67** *(10)*	**0.35** *(8)*	0.32 *(10)*	**0.15** *(0.3)*	**0.06** *(0.1)*
6 *LECR_RSS + LECR_NOISE*	1.38 *(1)*	0.70 *(4)*	0.36 *(3)*	**0.27** *(0.4)*	**0.15** *(0.2)*	0.08 *(0.1)*

4.4 Training and Estimation Time Performance

Table 3(a) presents the results of the measured delays for training using SVR and k-NN whereas table 3(b) presents the results of the measured delays for estimations. According to these numbers, the time taken by SVR to train can be very high. Hence, with *Dataset1* and the RSS metrics, the delays goes up to the tens of seconds. Then the time decreases with the use of smaller training sets. In the case of *k*-NN, no model are computed, the data are simply memorized. Therefore the training is very fast and essentially depends on the size of the training sets. As a consequence, *k*-NN values decrease geometrically by a factor of 2 when changing from *Dataset1* to *Dataset2* and then from *Dataset2* to *Dataset3*. According to section 2.1, SVR forces the estimated function to be within an ϵ distance of the averaged data, a requirement which can be tedious for the algorithm to fulfill. Hence, the high value for SVR model training are explained by the usage of this ϵ parameter which affects greatly the training accuracy as well as the delays. However, this affirmation would need more study focused on the SVR parameters and these specific data. The time taken for the estimation are higher when using SVR, than when using *k*-NN. The SNR delays vary with the size of the training set. This result seems unintuitive since SVR training model is based on regression. However, the results obtained with *k*-NN are conform to its training model which is based on the memorization of the entire training set. *k*-NN results are very good comparatively to the one of SVR. By observing the global results, we see that *k*-NN can largely compete with SVR when it comes to accuracy while at the same time being slightly faster.

5 Conclusions and Future Work

The main contribution presented in this paper deals with the design of a generic platform for monitoring and analyzing wireless networks. This wireless testbed is set in the RF protected environment of an anechoic room, allowing us to control the perturbation on the physical medium by generating noise. It also has the originality to integrate pure physical signal measurement tools as Lecroy oscilloscopes for very accurate measurements serving as ground truth. Based on the collected data, the second contribution of the paper deals with exhibiting the importance of PHY parameters on network communication performance. The correlation between the physical environment and the communication performance is so strong that it is possible by only monitoring the SNR and the RSS of the signal to predict the performance level at the TCP/IP level. This result has been demonstrated using different kinds of models, in particular the SVR and *k*-NN models presented in this paper. Future work includes a large exploitation of our platform. Indeed, for this preliminary stage, we just set simple scenarios with a single connection and simple noise model that can appear a bit far from realistic situations. These first simplistic scenarios were manadatory to validate the platform accuracy, and the monitoring and analysis tools, as well as for gaining the required skills required for this multi-thematic work, especially in the domain of the signal propagation and behaviour. We now plan to generate large datasets with more complex and realistic scenarios, and this for different kinds of wireless networks, including WIFI, UMTS, LTE, etc. We will also exploit this datasets by deeply analyzing them, understand how wireless networks behave, and then trying to improve the way we use and manage them.

Acknowledgments. This work is partially funded by the French National Research Agency (ANR) under two projects: the MAITRE project of the STIC AmSud program, and the RESCUE project of the VERSO program.

References

1. Vapnik, V., Golowich, S.E., Smola, A.: Support vector method for function approximation, regression estimation, and signal processing. In: Advances in Neural Information Processing Systems 9, vol. 9 (1997)
2. Wu, X., Kumar, V., Quinlan, J.R., Ghosh, J., Yang, Q., Motoda, H., McLachlan, G.J., Ng, A., Liu, B., Yu, P.S., Zhou, Z.-H., Steinbach, M., Hand, D.J., Steinberg, D.: Top 10 algorithms in data mining. Knowl. Inf. Syst. 14(1) (December 2007)
3. Claveirole, T., de Amorim, M.D.: Wipal and wscout, two hands-on tools for wireless packet traces manipulation and visualization. In: ACM Mobicom Workshop on Wireless Network Testbeds, Experimental Evaluation, and Characterization (2008)
4. Lecointre, A., Dragomirescu, D., Plana, R.: New methodology to design advanced mb-iruwb communication system. IEE Electronics Letters 11 (2008)
5. Raychaudhuri, D., Seskar, I., Ott, M., Ganu, S., Ramachandran, K., Kremo, H., Siracusa, R., Liu, H., Singh, M.: Overview of the orbit radio grid testbed for evaluation of next-generation wireless network protocols. In: 2005 IEEE Wireless Communications and Networking Conference, vol. 3, pp. 1664–1669 (2005)
6. Sapankevych, N., Sankar, R.: Time series prediction using support vector machines: A survey. IEEE Computational Intelligence Magazine 4(2), 24–38 (2009)
7. Smola, A.J., Schölkopf, B.: A tutorial on support vector regression. Statistics and Computing 14(3) (August 2004)
8. Altman, N.S.: An introduction to kernel and nearest-neighbor nonparametric regression. The American Statistician 46(3), 175–185 (1992), http://www.jstor.org/stable/2685209
9. Atkeson, C.G., Moore, A.W., Schaal, S.: Locally weighted learning. Artif. Intell. Rev. 11(1-5), 11–73 (1997), http://dx.doi.org/10.1023/A:1006559212014
10. Aamodt, A., Plaza, E.: Case-based reasoning: Foundational issues, methodological variations, and system approaches. AI Commun. 7(1), 39–59 (1994), http://dl.acm.org/citation.cfm?id=196108.196115
11. Pedregosa, F., Varoquaux, G., Gramfort, A., Michel, V., Thirion, B., Grisel, O., Blondel, M., Prettenhofer, P., Weiss, R., Dubourg, V., Vanderplas, J., Passos, A., Cournapeau, D., Brucher, M., Perrot, M., Duchesnay, E.: Scikit-learn: Machine learning in Python. Journal of Machine Learning Research 12, 2825–2830 (2011)

Gold Mining
in a River of Internet Content Traffic*

Zied Ben Houidi[1], Giuseppe Scavo[1], Samir Ghamri-Doudane[1],
Alessandro Finamore[2], Stefano Traverso[2], and Marco Mellia[2]

[1] Alcatel-Lucent Bell Labs, France
[2] Politecnico di Torino, Italy
{zied.ben_houidi,giuseppe.scavo1,samir.ghamri-doudane}@alcatel-lucent.com,
{finamore,traverso,mellia}@tlc.polito.it

Abstract. With the advent of Over-The-Top content providers (OTTs),
Internet Service Providers (ISPs) saw their portfolio of services shrink to
the low margin role of data transporters. In order to counter this effect,
some ISPs started to follow big OTTs like Facebook and Google in trying
to turn their data into a valuable asset. In this paper, we explore the
questions of what meaningful information can be extracted from network
data, and what interesting insights it can provide. To this end, we tackle
the first challenge of detecting "user-URLs", i.e., those links that were
clicked by users as opposed to those objects automatically downloaded by
browsers and applications. We devise algorithms to pinpoint such URLs,
and validate them on manually collected ground truth traces. We then
apply them on a three-day long traffic trace spanning more than 19,000
residential users that generated around 190 million HTTP transactions.
We find that only 1.6% of these observed URLs were actually clicked
by users. As a first application for our methods, we answer the question
of which platforms participate most in promoting the Internet content.
Surprisingly, we find that, despite its notoriety, only 11% of the user
URL visits are coming from Google Search.

1   Introduction

The Internet ecosystem has been historically composed only by two actors: *carriers* (e.g., ISPs) offering telephony services and Internet connectivity, and *end-users*. Recently, a new class of actors progressively gained a prime role: *Over-The-Top content and application providers* (OTTs [1]), i.e., third parties that are involved in the cross-domain distribution of content. Nowadays, this class of providers offers to end-users the same services that used to be offered by ISPs, plus a plethora of novel services. This is the case for instance of voice, texting and video services (e.g., Skype and Viber, WhatsApp and iMessage, or Netflix and YouTube).

---

* This work was supported by the European Commission under the FP7 IP Project
"An Intelligent Measurement Plane for Future Network and Application Management" (mPlane).

A. Dainotti, A. Mahanti, and S. Uhlig (Eds.): TMA 2014, LNCS 8406, pp. 91–103, 2014.

In this context, ISPs are more and more assuming the low profitable role of "bits carriers". To counter this effect, ISPs have been trying to find new added-value services that go beyond the traditional network connectivity business, investing in platforms to offer content [2] or cloud services [3,4].

However, one of the possible assets of an operator is the information about its customer-base. Some major ISPs such as AT&T and Verizon have recently investigated how to translate this asset into profit [5,6], for instance by re-selling customers' data to advertisement agencies as already done by other big OTTs such as Facebook and Google.

Extending this concept further, ISPs are thinking of leveraging the information their networks carry. By looking at the traffic that naturally flows, they have access to a humongous river from which possibly gold mining valuable information. This information could be used for at least two use cases. First, for web analytics/marketing purposes. Second, it can serve as an input for novel recommendation systems based on network traffic observation. And, differently from most[1] OTTs, ISPs have a unique vantage point that offers a wide-angle perspective, where multiple services and customers' habits are possibly exposed. They can try to exploit this unique vantage point respecting end-users privacy and regulations, for example, avoiding targeting single users, but considering aggregate information only.

Putting ourselves in the same position of an ISP observing the traffic in its network, we first address the technical issues related to i) how to identify the "contents" that users access from the enormous set of "objects" the network carries, and ii) how to pinpoint "interesting content" that is worth recommending out of the previous set. Second, we contrast the information that ISPs could get against the one OTTs have. This is instrumental to quantify if the ISPs are really in a more rewarding vantage point compared to the OTT position.

In this work we focus on HTTP traffic, the standard protocol used to transport web objects[2]. We consider all URL requests that are passively observed on a link of an ISP network. Immediately, we realize that the very large fraction of these URLs consists of requests automatically generated by browsers to fetch objects that are part of a web page (images, CSS files, JavaScript code, etc.), or by applications to poll automatic services (e.g., software update, chat keep-alive, etc.). We refer to these as *browser-URLs*. We are instead interested in the small subset of URLs that were intentionally visited by users, which we call *user-URLs*. Lot of ingenuity has to be used to extract this second subset, and, to the best of our knowledge, little work has been conducted in the literature, with few methodologies that are either obsolete for nowadays scenarios [7,8], or too complex for our needs [9],[10]. Our goal is to reach a good accuracy at identifying *user-URLs* using only HTTP requests, without the need to correlate them with corresponding responses.

---

[1] Google for instance observes a lot of visits thanks to its widespread Google analytics tool.

[2] We ignore HTTPS for now. A discussion about how to deal with possible encryption is given in Sec. 6.

Next, we address the problem of identifying *interesting-URLs*, i.e., those user-URLs that are possibly worth recommending in an eventual content promoting scenario. For instance, a popular news is worth being suggested, while the home-page of a home banking portal is less interesting.

To develop and validate our methodologies we use a set of ground truth traces collected by manually visiting the top 1,000 most popular web sites rated by Alexa and 1,000 news promoted by Google News. Then, we show the goodness of our methodologies with a three-day long HTTP traffic trace passively collected from a PoP of an European ISP.

Our major contributions are:

• We present a first set of algorithms and filtering stages to extract user-URLs from passive HTTP traces. We tune and quantify the performance of the algorithms using the dataset for which we have the ground truth. Our results show that we successfully detect 96% of user-URLs with only 1% of false positive rate and 66% of precision. Besides, precision can be enhanced to 80% with a loss of only 6% of user-URLs. When applied to the ISP trace, we found that only 1.6% of the 190 million HTTP requests in the dataset corresponds to actual URLs intentionally visited by users.

• We propose two algorithms to detect which user-URLs should be promoted also as interesting-URLs. Both algorithms leverage the social network information that is typically present in popular and interesting web sites. We found that only 15% of user-URLs may be classified as interesting-URLs.

• We show how rich the perspective of an ISP can be. We observe users accessing videos hosted on 9 different platforms, and news coming from 80 different news portals. This indicates that the view most OTTs get is different from the wide-angle picture an ISP could get. We further demonstrate this view by providing early web analytics results on the referral shares of well known content promotion platforms. We show that, surprisingly, only 11% of all user-URL views happened after (thanks to) a Google Search, and, in the best case, no more than 13% of them came from Facebook, Twitter or Google News.

The rest of this paper is organized as follows. First, Sec. 2 describes the background and resumes the related work of this paper. Second, Sec. 3 describes the datasets we use. Sec. 4 describes our algorithms and presents their performance evaluation. Sec. 4 applies our filtering methods on real data. Finally, Sec. 6 presents the open problems of this work and concludes the paper.

2   Background and Related Work

The structure of a web page has considerably grown in complexity in the last decade. Today, it often consists of a complicated tangle of HTML, JavaScript, multimedia objects, CSS, XML files, etc. As depicted in Fig. 1, when attempting to view a web page, the browser downloads each of these objects using separate HTTP requests. As a consequence, a simple user's click on a URL generates a cascade of several HTTP requests between the user terminal and

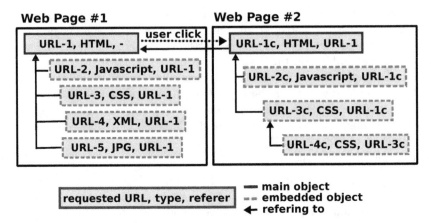

Fig. 1. Sequence of HTTP requests when accessing some standard web pages

an almost unpredictable number of servers and caches that store these objects. Besides, JavaScript, Ajax and Flash objects may generate extra HTTP traffic that was not intentionally requested by the user (e.g., the automatic fetching of a YouTube video). Furthermore, many non-web applications nowadays rely on HTTP to exchange their data (e.g., Dropbox and software updates). Therefore, even when a trace of HTTP transactions performed by a terminal is available, identifying which requests actually correspond to a human interaction is not a straightforward task.

To the best of our knowledge, only few methods have been proposed in the literature to detect URLs that were intentionally visited by users [8],[7],[9],[10].

The first method is time-based [8], it relies on the intuition that a cascade of browser-URLs follows the initial user-URL. Browser-URLs are tightly grouped in time after the user-URL request has been observed (see red dotted boxes in Fig. 1). As such, the first request after a given inactivity period can be considered as a new user-URL, while all the following HTTP requests happening before a time threshold are assumed to be browser-URLs. Unfortunately the estimation of the algorithm time thresholds is not a straightforward task, and many factors (e.g., latencies due to network conditions) may harm the performance of this method [9].

Another methodology, presented in [7], is type-based. It relies on the media information reported in the *Content-Type* field contained in the HTTP responses: the URLs associated to responses specifying text/HTML type are considered as main pages while the others are considered as browser-URLs. However, this approach has been shown to be unreliable [11].

To the best of our knowledge, the most recent methodologies to investigate the composition of modern web pages are StreamStructure [9] and ReSurf [10]. They both exploit the *Referer*[3] field to split HTTP transactions into multiple streams, thus reducing the temporal overlaps between clicks on different URLs (e.g., when a user keeps several tabs open in her browser, for the same time

---

[3] A field in the HTTP GET request that specifies from which previous page the URL has been referred.

window the technique can identify different streams). StreamStructure processes each detected stream separately. On each of them, it first applies a type-based filter (based on Content-Type) to keep only HTML/text pages. It then applies a time-based filter to detect main pages. To set a proper time threshold, the method leverages the Google Analytics beacon: once the Google Analytics beacon is downloaded, the page is considered as loaded, so that there is no need to set a static time threshold. Despite the improvements, StreamStructure still suffer from some limitations. First, it leverages Google Analytics information, which is present in only 40% of web pages (according to [9], [10]). Furthermore, it relies on the HTTP Content-Type field which has two drawbacks: (1) it has been shown to be often unreliable [11] and (2) this needs to monitor both HTTP requests and corresponding responses, which increases the complexity of the traffic extraction phase . We target a solution that overcomes these drawbacks, and for which only outgoing network traffic is needed to be monitored, so that the traffic extraction and filtering are kept as simple as possible. More recently, ReSurf [10] has been proposed. Although it does a great job in overcoming the limitations of [9], it still rely on the Content-Type (as well as the Content-Size), which makes it inadequate for our needs.

3   Datasets

While per-object information is sufficient to study caching (e.g., assess caching policies and gains) or filtering (e.g., blocking unwanted objects), further processing is needed to infer human-induced HTTP transactions. This is one of the challenges that we tackle in this paper. For this purpose, we rely on two types of traces. The first is collected in a controlled test-bed where the ground truth is known and used. The second corresponds to a real traffic trace on which we apply our algorithms to appreciate the type of information that is possible to extract.

For the preliminary evaluation of our methods, we collect two ground truth traces. First, similarly to [9], [10], we build a trace (*HTTP-Alexa*) by manually visiting the top 100 most popular web sites according to Alexa ranking. In each of these sites, we randomly visit up to 10 links contained in them. We manually collect all the clicked URLs as they were reported by the browser bar. In parallel, we capture and extract HTTP requests generated by the browser. This resulted in a total list of 905 user-URLs, corresponding to 39025 browser-URLs. Second, we build a similar trace (*HTTP-GNews*) by visiting around 900 news sites promoted on Google News.

For the real data, we use the open-source traffic monitoring tool Tstat [12] to rebuild HTTP conversations. Thanks to this tool, we obtained a three-day long HTTP traffic trace, *HTTP-ISP*, which we collected at a vantage point of a commercial ISP network. The dataset contains the HTTP requests generated by about 19,000 residential customers. In total we observed more than 190 millions of HTTP requests.

4   Content Filtering Algorithms

In this section, we introduce and evaluate our web object filtering algorithms. First, we aim at distinguishing between intentionally visited URLs, i.e., user-URLs, and automatically requested ones, i.e., browser-URLs.

4.1   Identification of User-URLs

As explained in Sec. 2, we believe that new and simpler methods must be devised to identify user-URLs. As a design choice, we assume the ability to parse only HTTP requests to reduce the complexity at the probe capturing the traffic and the amount of data to process. To this end, we propose four filtering mechanisms and compare their performance as detailed below.

1) F-Referer: This method exploits the *Referer* field, not to separate requests in different streams as done in [9], [10], but to directly pinpoint user-URLs. As shown in Fig. 1, when the URL of a web page is clicked, a sequence of HTTP requests is generated by the browser to retrieve all the embedded objects, thus generating a cascade of browser-URLs. All these requests have as a referer the starting user-URL (see Fig. 1). Therefore, for each request, this filter ignores the URL and focuses on the *referer* field, so that we are sure of capturing all the original user-URLs. However, observe that this approach captures all web objects with a hierarchical structure (e.g., JavaScript and CSS files that embed themselves other files).

2) F-Children: The nowadays trend of web page design goes towards including lots of embedded objects, which we call *children*. By counting the number of URLs seen with a given referer, it is possible to know the number of children composing the corresponding parent URL. Thus, we can filter out those URLs with a low number of children, e.g., simple objects that contain few other objects (e.g., URL-3c in Fig. 1).

3) F-Type: Similar in spirit to [7], this filter acts on URLs based on their type. However, instead of relying on the *Content-Type* field which is exposed in HTTP responses, we inspect the extensions of the objects queried by the HTTP requests: we discard URLs pointing to *.js, .css, .swf* objects.

4) F-Ad: A large amount of advertisement is embedded in nowadays web pages through the mean of iframe HTML nodes. By design, an advertisement iframe may embed several other objects itself that has as referer the advertisement page. Thus, ads likely to pass all above filters. To counter this phenomenon, we blacklist URLs pointing to known advertisement platforms using the filter provided by AdBlock [13].

In addition to these methods, we also test a time-based filter (F-Time) as proposed in [8], [9], [10], using a static time threshold.

Performance on Ground Truth Datasets. We first evaluate these methods on the *HTTP-Alexa* dataset, described in Sec. 3. In Fig. 2 we graphically

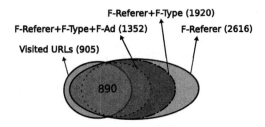

Fig. 2. Venn diagram reporting the effects of different filtering methods on our *HTTP-Alexa* dataset

report the performance of filters F-Referer alone, F-Referer + F-Type and F-Referer + F-Type + F-Ad through a Venn diagram. We observe that the F-Referer method alone has a high "filtering capacity". In fact, it reduces the set of browser-URLs from the 39025 URLs in *HTTP-Alexa* to only 2616 candidate user-URLs. It has therefore a 4,4% of false positive rate (FPR)[4]. Besides, it has a high *recall*[5] (98,34%). Manually inspecting the few misses, we find that they either correspond to HTTPS visits which did not pass the referer field, or to Flash content for which no URL requests are issued for browsing. However, its precision[6] is still low (34%), which means that there is still a considerable amount of false positives. To reduce the set of false positives, we combine the F-Referer filter with the other filters with different configurations, i.e., considering different thresholds. The results are summarized in Tab. 1. Both F-Time and F-Children enhance the precision when we increase respectively the time threshold and the minimum number of children (they invalidate false positives). However, they come at the cost of decreasing the recall (invalidating valid user-URLs). On the other hand, the F-Type and the F-Ad filters let us enhance the precision, with almost no impact on the recall. In reality, the F-Ad filter removes 16 valid user-URLs (see the dark green slice that is cut by the introduction of F-Ad in Fig. 2), but these were unintentionally visited when we collected the trace[7].

We acknowledge that there is a tradeoff between recall and precision. The best combination to apply depends therefore on whether we want to capture all user-URLs or to remove all false positives. As a start, we opt for now for a most conservative approach that favors recall over precision. For the rest of the paper, we retain the F-Type coupled with F-Ad filters applied after the F-Referer method (i.e., F-Referer + F-Type + F-Ad). This guarantees 96.57% of recall, with only 1.17% of false positive rate.

---

[4] Number of False Positives (here 1711) over the number of negatives (here 38120).

[5] Number of URLs correctly labeled as user-URLs (true positives, here 890) over the number of user-URLs (ground truth, here 905).

[6] Number of true positives over the number of items labeled as positive by the method (here 2616).

[7] Although we acknowledge that some advertisements might interest people, we decide to skip them for now.

Table 1. Performance of different filtering combinations

Method	Recall	Precision	FPR
F-Ref + F-Time (0.01s)	97.90%	37.67%	3.7%
F-Ref + F-Time (0.1s)	96.13%	41.09%	3.17%
F-Ref + F-Time (1s)	87.51%	55.15%	1.39%
F-Ref + F-Children (remove <= 1)	94.8%	43.13%	2.84%
F-Ref + F-Children (remove <= 2)	93.14%	49.76%	2.06%
F-Ref + F-Type	98.34%	46.35%	2.66%
F-Ref + F-Ad	96.57%	44.14%	2.82%
F-Ref + F-Type + F-Ad	**96.57%**	**66.41%**	**1.17%**
F-Ref + F-Type + F-Ad + F-Children (remove <= 2)	91.82%	77.08%	0.45%
F-Ref + F-Type + F-Ad + F-Children (remove <= 3)	89%	79.1%	0.29%

4.2 Pinpointing Interesting URLs via OSN Metadata

With the goal of targeting a recommendation system, we are now interested in identifying interesting-URLs among the detected user-URLs. Indeed, manually looking we find that many of them do not correspond to URLs that might attract users' attention (e.g., the web portal of an online bank). Therefore, an extra step in the filtering is needed to go from user-URLs to *interesting-URLs*.

Finding a measure of interest is challenging since it involves human subjects and tastes. We investigate on simple heuristics that leverages online social network meta-information. We assume that interesting URLs should be rich with "social" features (e.g., share buttons). The idea is that if a web page is meant to be shared, then it might interest other people. We thus develop two methods to understand which user-URLs are "social-networks enabled". In particular we considered two approaches:

1) Active: This method uses a web scraper to actively query the URL and parse the returned HTML code looking for the presence of the OpenGraph protocol[8] [14]. If the protocol is present, the user-URL is classified as interesting.

2) Passive: This approach aims at passively detecting if a web page contains any of the well known social networks buttons. Given a user-URL X, we inspect its children, i.e., URLs having X as referer, and match them against a list of URLs necessary to load such buttons[9]. Such list was built by following the web development guidelines of several different social networks.

Performance on Ground Truth Datasets. To evaluate these methods, we test if they already work on platforms that are known to be "interesting". In particular, we test them against Google News. For this purpose, we visit 1000 URLs promoted by Google News. Applying the active and the passive methods on this trace, we find that they classify as interesting respectively 79% and 70.72% of Google News URLs. For the active method, this means that 79% of Google news URLs actually implement the OpenGraph protocol. To understand the passive method's false negatives, we manually inspect them. We find that

---

[8] The OpenGraph protocol was developed by Facebook to help web pages getting integrated in "the social graph".

[9] Available at http://www.retitlc.polito.it/finamore/plugins.txt.

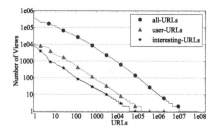

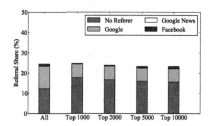

Fig. 3. Content items popularity before and after filtering (*HTTP-ISP*)

Fig. 4. Referral shares for user-URLs

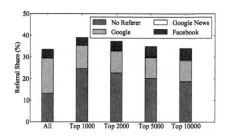

Fig. 5. Referral shares for interesting-URLs

they correspond to web sites that use custom methods to embed the social networks buttons and that our filter fails to identify. For instance, YouTube uses a non standard solution. However, since it is OpengGraph compliant, our active method correctly detects it. To estimate the capability of pinpointing interesting web objects, we first apply the filter chain F-Referer + F-Type + F-Ad on *HTTP-Alexa* trace to detect user-URLs; then we use our social-aware heuristics. Intuitively, the URLs Alexa ranking are less likely to be promoted than the Google News URLs, we expect them therefore to contain much less interesting URLs. This was confirmed by our both methods which gave similar results: 33% of the user-URLs were labeled as interesting-URLs using the active method, and 35% using the passive one.

These methods look promising, we use them in the rest of the paper and leave their enhancement for future work.

5 Applying the Filtering on Real Data

In this section, we apply our filtering methods on the real data (*HTTP-ISP*) with two purposes in mind: first to rank and analyze user-URLs and interesting-URLs, and second to do some preliminary web analytics job.

5.1 Additional Problems

When considering the real HTTP traffic for filtering, some additional sources of error have been detected and called for more ingenuity. In particular, we noticed two main problems, and we propose two simple mechanisms to factor them out.

i) URLs generated by non-browser applications: Most applications use HTTP to automatically download web objects. The queried URLs are clearly not relevant, and must be ignored. We identify those URLs by inspecting the *User-Agent* field, which informs about which client application generated the HTTP request, and white-listing well-known browsers only. This discards around 15% of URL requests in our dataset.

ii) Inflated popularity induced by some users: Sometimes browsers generate multiple HTTP requests for the same content, e.g., automatically reloading a page, or downloading videos in chunks. This phenomenon inflates the popularity of some URLs. We counter this effect by counting a URL only once for each user-id.

5.2   Ranking and Classifying URLs

We first apply the F-Referer + F-Type + F-Ad filters, and study the popularity of the resulting user-URLs. Fig. 3 shows the popularity of all-URLs, user-URLs and interesting-URLs. The x-axis reports the rank of URLs, while the y-axis reports the actual number of occurrences of each URL, i.e., its popularity. Both axes are log-scale. Observe that the distribution follows a typical Zipf law, and many URLs show a low popularity: only 10,000 out of millions URLs have a popularity larger than 1000.

As expected, the user-URLs represent a tiny fraction of all the URLs. Our method detects that among the 190 million URL requests, only 1,6% correspond to actual user-URLs requests. Among these user-URLs views, only around 15% were detected as potentially interesting.

We next analyze the interesting user-URLs. We manually classify the top 1000 URLs to build a set of rules to help us having a preliminary classification of the rest of the URLs. Among these top 1000 URLs, we find that 482 are news (or blogs), 336 are services (e.g., online shops, travel engines, etc.) and 91 were videos. Extending a similar classification on the rest of the interesting user-URLs, we find that (at least) 18% correspond to videos coming from 9 different platforms (YouTube alone 15%) and 22% correspond to news from around 80 different news web sites. This observation confirms that the ISP is probably the only entity that has such a rich cross-service and wide-angle vantage point on the Internet.

Open Issues. We now report some of the limits observed with our filtering methods. First, for the user-URLs, although we drastically reduce the set of candidate URLs, our results still contain some false positives, which is not surprising given their relative high percentage. This is mainly due to the complex composition of web pages with a nested structure of objects. In the future, we plan to (1) test some of our other filtering methods that favor precision at the cost of recall (example the children method) as well as (2) work on enhancing our methods.

Another issue is that the returned list of the top most interesting-URLs contains popular and well-known web pages, e.g., the Google Search home page, or the most popular news portals. This confirms on the one hand the goodness of our algorithms; on the other hand, this opens the space for smarter algorithms to pinpoint interesting-but-not-obvious-URLs.

Finally, our algorithms outperform Resurf [10] in terms of processing speed. Applying F-Ref + F-Type + F-ad on one hour of *HTTP-ISP* (19,000 users) took us around 43 minutes. This is about the same time it took Resurf to process one hour traffic of only 1,000 users. However, our main bottleneck is the F-Ad due to the large size of its catalog; F-Ref + F-Type alone take only 3 minutes to complete. We plan to optimize it as part of our future work.

5.3   Early Web Analytics Results

Web analytics is an important tool for business and market research. It helps companies to refine the target of their advertisement campaigns, eventually giving precious hints about where to place advertisement to collect more user clicks. Most of such tools today work on a per site basis: each site has a local view on where its visits came from (referring to it). Thus, a general view is missing, and it is not clear which web platforms drive most of today's user visits. Thanks to our filtering methods, ISPs overcome this limit, reaching a cross-service view, by simply inspecting the referers associated to the detected URLs.

As a preliminary step, we start by quantifying the referral share of Google, Facebook and Google News, i.e. how many visits are driven thanks to these promotion platforms. We report our results in Fig. 4 and Fig. 5, for user-URLs and interesting-URLs, respectively. The y-axis reports the referral share in percentage over all the views in the 3 days. In the x-axis, we apply the results on different populations of URLs depending on their popularity. The "No Referer" shares correspond to URLs which had no referer (e.g., due to direct browsing, bookmarks, email, etc.).

Interestingly, a considerable amount of visits came with no referer (around 13%). This goes up to 25% for the top 1000 interesting-URLs, meaning that direct browsing is common when browsing the web. As expected, the shares of visits driven by well-known platforms are larger for interesting-URLs compared to user-URLs. However, the share of requests coming from Google is more important for unpopular objects if compared to popular ones. This is again expected since users use search engines to look for unknown content rather than popular links. However, it is surprising that despite their notoriety, the referral shares of these platforms are relatively low: Only 11% of user URLs visits came from Google (and only 16% for interesting-URLs). Observe that the rest of the shares correspond to other platforms, such as news portals and blogs. We intend to rank them as part of our future work.

Open Issues. One of the main issues that we figured out in this study is due to usage of HTTPS. In fact, when going from a page served over HTTPS to another served over HTTP, the standard imposes to not include the referer field [15], so that users' privacy is preserved. However, because of its importance to marketers, many websites implement workarounds, either by using the meta referer or HTTP redirections, to still inform the landing page where the visit came from. This biases our results inflating the "No Referer" share with visits that came from HTTPS pages, and for which the referer was not passed. To get a hint on the consistency of our results concerning Google and Facebook (that both use HTTPS for browsing), we made experiments employing several popular web browsers and different operating systems. We visited URLs starting from Google Search and Facebook and check whether the referer was correctly passed. For Google, we found that the referer is always passed, but this does not always hold for Facebook, indeed we observed different behaviors depending on the browser and operating system. As a consequence, the Facebook referral shares are underestimated, but upper bounded by the "No Referer" share. We plan to investigate more this issue as part of our future work.

6   Conclusions, Open Problems and Future Work

Driven by the intuition that ISPs have a great deal of information at their disposal that can be extracted from passive observation of the traffic flowing in their networks, we propose in this paper a set of algorithms to extract popular URLs from real Internet traffic. In this study we analyzed the feasibility of the automatic extraction of useful/interesting URLs from the humongous amount of HTTP data that flows through an ISP-wide network. Other challenges must be clearly faced, and ingenuity must be used to find appropriate solutions:

i) Users' privacy: tracking users' activity is (commonly) performed by OTT providers and it has been strongly criticized recently [16]. ISPs face similar issues. They are allowed to monitor traffic for troubleshooting or even marketing purposes. Data could even be stored if properly anonymized and/or aggregated, i.e., if user's identity is irreversibly hidden. Our algorithms monitor aggregated data by design, without the need to offend users' privacy.

ii) Traffic encryption: Apart the issue discussed in Sec. 5.3, traffic encryption deeply hampers whatever traffic mining operation. This is not a negligible aspect since today more than 20% of the HTTP traffic is encrypted [17]. Mining interesting URLs in presence of encrypted traffic is another interesting research direction. However, end-customers could be involved directly, e.g., offering them personalized services (such as media curation, or parental control filters) in exchange for installing some plugins that collect clicks.

Our preliminary results suggest that the extraction of user-URLs from network traffic is a challenging task given the structure of nowadays web pages. However, "network gold mining" may represent a promising opportunity for ISPs to compete with OTTs in front of marketers and advertisers. Moreover, we believe information provided by our methodologies can be employed for a broad gamma of applications, ranging from new passive recommendation services to caching systems and parental control tools to name a few. In our ongoing efforts, we are developing each presented algorithm to run in a complete online extraction system, capable of working in a real ISP network scenario.

References

1. York, D.: What is an over-the-top (ott) application or service? (July 2012), http://goo.gl/vmxVT
2. Telecom italia vod, http://www.cubovision.it/
3. At&t cloud service, https://www.synaptic.att.com/clouduser/
4. Telefonica cloud service, http://www.telefonica.com/en/digital/html/digital_services/cloud.shtml
5. At&t joins verizon, facebook in selling customer data, http://goo.gl/FGDEp6
6. Kleinman, A.: Verizon selling customers' cell phone data: Report, http://goo.gl/RVAEAV (November 2013)
7. Choi, H.-K., Limb, J.O.: A behavioral model of web traffic. In: IEEE ICNP, Toronto, CA (1999)
8. Barford, P., Crovella, M.: Generating representative web workloads for network and server performance evaluation. In: ACM SIGMETRICS, Madison, US-WI (1998)
9. Ihm, S., Pai, V.S.: Towards understanding modern web traffic. In: ACM IMC, Berlin, DE (2011)
10. Xie, G., Iliofotou, M., Karagiannis, T., Faloutsos, M., Jin, Y.: Resurf: Reconstructing web-surfing activity from network traffic. In: IFIP Networking Conference (2013)
11. Schneider, F., Ager, B., Maier, G., Feldmann, A., Uhlig, S.: Pitfalls in HTTP traffic measurements and analysis. In: Taft, N., Ricciato, F. (eds.) PAM 2012. LNCS, vol. 7192, pp. 242–251. Springer, Heidelberg (2012)
12. Finamore, A., Mellia, M., Meo, M., Munafò, M.M., Rossi, D.: Experiences of Internet traffic monitoring with Tstat. In: IEEE Network (2011)
13. Adblock Plus, http://easylist.adblockplus.org/ (July 2013)
14. Facebook OpenGraph, http://goo.gl/2y2VN
15. Fielding, R., Gettys, J., Mogul, J., Frystyk, H., Masinter, L., Leach, P., Berners-Lee, T.: Hypertext transfer protocol–http/1.1, 1999. RFC2616 (2006)
16. Akkus, I.E., Chen, R., Hardt, M., Francis, P., Gehrke, J.: Non-tracking web analytics. In: ACM CCS, Raleigh, US-NC (2012)
17. Finamore, A., Gehlen, V., Mellia, M., Munafo, M., Nicolini, S.: The need for an intelligent measurement plane: The example of time-variant cdn policies. In: IEEE NETWORKS, Rome, IT (2012)

The Rise of Panopticons: Examining Region-Specific Third-Party Web Tracking

Marjan Falahrastegar[1], Hamed Haddadi[1], Steve Uhlig[1], and Richard Mortier[2]

[1] Queen Mary University of London
[2] University of Nottingham

Abstract. Today's web has a huge, diverse ecosystem of third-party websites collecting information about users and providing them with content such as targeted advertisements. In this paper we study this ecosystem of third-party websites. We sample every continent, targeting the 500 most popular websites in the US, UK, Australia, China, Egypt, Iran and Syria. This allows us to contrast the commonplace, western-dominated views of the web with less studied countries. We find 2,097 third-party web services, reflecting the diversity of services and types of application/content they involve, e.g., advertisement, ad trackers, CDNs, news, sport, and pornography. We find those third-party web services offering ad tracking services to be the most prevalent. In addition to the usual suspects (e.g., DoubleClick and Google), we find a rich ecosystem of *local* third-party websites that are country and language dependent.

1 Introduction

The role of the Internet in everyday life evolves continuously. Online Social Networks (OSNs), streaming videos, and online shopping are all now daily activities in the lives of most netizens. In addition, web interactions afforded by developments such as dynamic client-side interaction (e.g., Ajax [1]) and cloud-based services [2] have lead to significant changes in the Internet traffic [3] and website complexity [4].

One of the expanding family of new entrants in the Web ecosystem are the third-party tracking services and cookies. They provide features such as advertising, analytics, OSN plugins, and user tracking and profiling. Although some user interactions with these services may be conscious and explicit, e.g., sharing content or clicking *like* on various OSNs, most interactions users have with these services will not be explicit and indeed, users may often be unaware of the presence of the services at all. The increasing trade of personal information between these services and their increasing ubiquity and ability to track users from one page to the next, often on different websites, is a major source of concerns about privacy.

A number of recent works have investigated the effect of these third-party services in terms of the performance [4], privacy [5] and transparency [6] challenges they introduce. In this paper we study the presence of third-party services across the most popular websites in different regions of the world when viewed from the

A. Dainotti, A. Mahanti, and S. Uhlig (Eds.): TMA 2014, LNCS 8406, pp. 104–114, 2014.

vantage point of an individual user. We measure the prevalence of these services in the modern web, focusing on a few distinct but key countries in both the East and the West. Our measurements are taken from a single vantage point and are thus not based on user interactions with these websites in the countries in question. As DNS may redirect users from different regions to different servers, whose version of the webpage point to different third parties, one may observe different third parties than in our dataset. In this paper our specific contributions are as follows:

- We find a surprisingly large ecosystem of third-party sites: within just the 500 most popular websites, according to Alexa,[1] in the 7 countries we examine, we find 2,097 unique third party websites.
- We categorise these third-party websites based on the nature of the service they provide (ad trackers, Content Distribution Networks (CDNs), analytics services, OSNs, etc.) and we find that advertisement and ad trackers make the bulk of the third-party websites in their number. The prevalence of user tracking services (ad trackers, analytics and trackers) and their ubiquity across a broad portfolio of popular websites allow the corporations behind them to obtain a rich, detailed view of individuals' browsing behaviour, trends, interests and correlations between activities.
- Surprisingly, third-party CDNs are only the third category by number, despite capturing about half of all referrals from the origin websites. The CDN market therefore appears more consolidated than that for user tracking services. In addition to ad networks, trackers, and CDNs, we observe a rich ecosystem of other third-party sites that reflect specific user interests, activities and applications, e.g., sports, shopping, OSNs, porn, and gaming.

2   Method

We investigate the presence of third-party websites in a diverse set of countries by analysing the landing pages of popular websites in seven countries. We use the Alexa top-500 ranking per-country to determine the popular websites for each country. In this paper we present data from five countries representing each continent (the USA, the UK, Australia, China and Egypt), and from an additional two countries (Iran, Syria) as samples of less commonly-studied countries with a common language (Arabic).

We identify presence of a third-party site in a given landing page using a combination of the *domain* and *adns* approaches from Krishnamurthy & Wills [5]. Thus we identify a third-party site as one whose second-level domain and authoritative DNS server differ from the second-level domain name and authoritative DNS server of the origin site. Use of the authoritative DNS server in this way enables us to correctly classify cases such as bbc.co.uk and bbci.co.uk, where each belongs to the same company even though the second-level domain names are different.

---

[1] http://www.alexa.com/

We automated this process with (*i*) a Python script that fetches the landing pages from a given list of sites, (*ii*) a Chrome extension that detected third-party websites based on the *domain* approach, and (*iii*) a Python script that carried out the *ADNS* approach. The initial script opens the landing page of the current target site in a Chrome browser a website in a browser tab. While the landing page is open on the Chrome, the extension monitors all HTTP requests sent by the browsed website and identifies third-party requests as those where the second-level domain name of the URL differs from the second-level domain name of the origin website. The list of third-party requests corresponding to each origin site is recorded in a log file. The ADNS server name of the obtained third-party requests and their origin site were fetched using `nslookup -type=soa` command available on Linux. Subsequently, the requests were compared against each other to refine those cases where two second-level domain names are different while one is an alias for the other one. Every 20 seconds the next site is fetched and its landing page is analysed as explained above.

We carried out this procedure once in October 2013 for each country, from a single PC, with Linux OS, located in the UK. We are currently extending the set of countries considered and investigating the possibility of running this process from within different countries to gain further insight into the prevalence of the local third-party websites.

3   Third-Party Presence in the WWW

In this section we describe our collected data and analyse the presence of third-party websites in the dataset. We retrieved a total of 2,104 unique websites that involved at least one third-party website. The origin site that referred to the most third-party websites was `free-tv-video-online.me`, a popular video hosting website in the US (Alexa rank 305), which issues 1,501 calls to 135 third-party sites. We identified 2,759 unique sites as third-party based on the *domain* approach, which reduced by 24% to 2,097 when the *adns* approach was applied. In total third-party sites were referred to 119,911 times across the entire dataset. A majority of third-party sites, 1,063 (51%), were referred to fewer than 5 times. However, a small number, 37 (1.8%), are very popular and referred to by more than 500 of the 2,104 websites we studied.

Figure 1, 2 provides the cumulative distribution of the identified third-party sites across different countries. Examining each country individually, we see that the English language countries (US, GB, Australia; Figure 1(a)) are all very close together, indicating similar prevalence of third-party services in these countries (although the specific third-party services may differ). However, the other countries studied (Egypt, China, Iran, Syria; Figure 1(b), 2) display quite marked differences, with only Arabic language countries (Egypt and Syria) being similar. This suggests that the prevalence of tracking does differ between different countries with different languages.

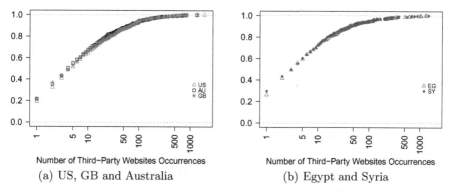

(a) US, GB and Australia   (b) Egypt and Syria

Fig. 1. The cumulative distribution of third-party websites in each country

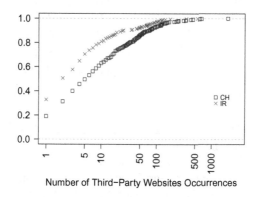

Number of Third–Party Websites Occurrences

Fig. 2. The cumulative distribution of third-party websites in Iran and China

3.1   Role of Third-Party Websites

Third-party websites provide three main services: (*i*) advertisement, (*ii*) content delivery via CDNs and (*iii*) tracking user activity across websites. Given the prevalence of these third-party sites, we want to understand the relative importance of each category in this ecosystem.

We identified the category of each third-party website by combining three methods. First, we used information from the Abine website[2] to detect ad-trackers, trackers, and analytic sites. Second, we examined the third-party domain name itself for presence of keywords indicating the category. Finally, we manually categorised any remaining third-party websites in the top-300 (approximately 130 required manual categorisation).

Table 1 presents a breakdown of the 28% (681 websites including top-300 from every country) of the third-party websites that were categorised.[3] For each

---

[2] https://www.abine.com

[3] This extends previous work [4] where just 200 third-party websites were categorised.

Table 1. Categorisation of third-party websites

No.	Category Name	(Code)	Number Total	(%)	Referrals Total	(%)	Median
1	Advertising	(A)	192	(28%)	4073	(4%)	6.0
2	Ad trackers	(D)	141	(21%)	36768	(35%)	88.0
3	CDN	(C)	88	(13%)	17198	(16%)	28
4	Analysts	(Y)	68	(10%)	22081	(21%)	54.5
5	Web hosting	(W)	46	(6%)	2232	(2%)	8.5
6	Trackers	(T)	41	(6%)	7641	(7%)	35.0
7	News	(N)	29	(4%)	684	(0.7%)	3.0
8	Shopping	(S)	17	(2%)	1135	(1%)	64
9	Portal	(R)	12	(2%)	1094	(1%)	93.5
10	Sport News	(E)	9	(1%)	354	(0.3%)	4.0
11	Porn	(P)	8	(1%)	1811	(2%)	238.5
12	OSN	(O)	8	(1%)	6667	(6%)	67.5
13	Video hosting	(V)	7	(1%)	790	(0.8%)	120.0
14	Game	(G)	5	(0.7%)	354	(0.3%)	4.0
15	Other	(X)	10	(1%)	1213	(1%)	79

category we give both the number of third-party websites and the number of referrals to them from the origin websites.

The largest category of observed third-party sites is *advertisement*. Websites in this category provide general advertisement services such as ad design. The second biggest category is *ad trackers*, sites that facilitate targeted advertisement by profiling user online activities across different websites. Other categories that also profile user behaviour include *analysts* and *trackers*, in forth and sixth places respectively. Overall, we find that about 37% of categorised third-party sites track user behaviour.

It is worth noting that, despite the large number of advertisement third-party websites, this is not the most prevalent category in terms of referrals, i.e., in terms of the use by origin sites of third-parties within the category. *Ad trackers* and *analysis* are the most frequently referred categories amongst with CDNs, delivering content such as images or scripts on behalf of the origin websites, placed third. Although there are far fewer sites in categories such as OSNs or porn, the proportion of referrals is nearer the larger categories and, in the case of OSNs is larger than the top category, *advertising*.

3.2   Third-Party Websites across Countries

In this section we investigate the distribution of third-party websites across the US, Great Britain (GB), Australia (AU), China (CH), Egypt (EG), Iran (IR) and Syria (SY).

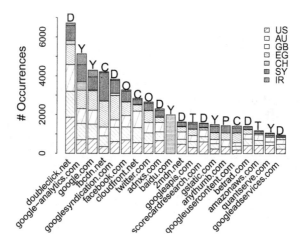

Fig. 3. Top 20 third-party websites with the most referrals from origin websites in the dataset for US, AU, GB, CH, EG, IR and SY. The categories of these third-party websites are indicated by the letter codes provided in Table 1.

Figure 3 shows the distribution of referrals to the top 20 third-party websites per country. The most popular third-party site is `DoubleClick.net` with 6,713 referrals from 2,104 origin sites. DoubleClick is a third-party ad tracker that records user activities across all sites subscribed to its service. This was the most frequently referred to third-party site in the US and was least frequently referred to in China and Iran. Google Analytics was the next most referred to third-party site, and actually obtained a larger share of referrals than DoubleClick from the Iranian and Chinese websites. Overall, Google properties dominate the top-20 by referrals occupying positions #1, #2, #3, #5, #13, #15, #17, and #20.

In general, the prevalence of third-party sites differs strikingly in China and Iran compared to the other countries studied. However, for example, the position of `Baidu.com` among Chinese websites is similar to DoubleClick among top 500 websites in the US. Baidu is a search engine specialised for Chinese-language queries. It was referred to by 207 unique websites from gaming sites (e.g., `61.com`) to news sites (e.g., `tiexue.net`).

In general, the way that top websites in Arabic speaking countries (Egypt and Syria) refer to third-party sites is similar to the top websites in the English-speaking countries (US, Great Britain, Australia) apart from `fbcdn.net`, a Facebook property. This was referred to about 1,400 times from the popular sites of Egypt and Syria, about 3.8 times more than from the US. Indeed, Facebook is the most popular website in Egypt and Syria, while it ranks third in the US, Great Britain and Australia based on the Alexa records for October 2013.

We next look at the top 20 third-party sites across countries with a common language, i.e., English (US, Great Britain, Australia), Arabic (Egypt and Syria), Persian (Iran) and Chinese (China).[4] Figure 4 shows that there are just two

---

[4] We ignore differences in regional variants of English, as well as the many different regional languages in China.

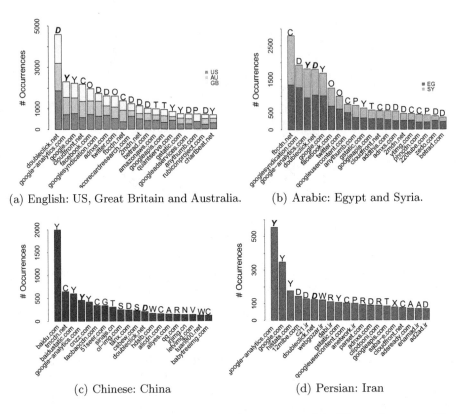

Fig. 4. The top 20 third-party websites in the countries with different language. The categories of these third-party websites are indicated by the letter codes provided in table 1. Those common to all countries are in *Italic Bold*.

common third-party websites among all the countries (DoubleClick and Google Analytics), while there are seven in common among the English, Arabic and Persian groups.

3.3 Regional Third-Party Websites

We now examine if some third-party websites appear exclusively in a specific group of countries. Table 2 shows the top-20 third-party websites in each country. In our data, 125 unique third-party websites appear in the top websites of English-language countries (US, AU, GB) but do not appear at all in the top-20 of other countries (CH, EG, IR, SY). The top-20 that fall in this situation are shown in Figure 5. These third-party websites were referred to by 133 unique sites such as groupon.co.uk (shopping website), usnews.net (news website). On the other hand, there are 30 unique third-party sites that appear only in Arabic-language countries (SY, EG). The top 20 of these third-party websites are provided in Figure 5.

Table 2. Top 20 third-party websites amongst popular websites of each country of our dataset. Those common to all countries are in **bold**. The categories of these third-party websites are indicated by the letter codes provided in table 1.

USA	Great Britain	Australia	China	Egypt	Iran	Syria
(D) double click.net	**(D) double click.net**	**(D) double click.net**	(Y) baidu.com	(C) fbcdn.net	**(Y) google analytics .com**	(C) fbcdn.net
(Y) google.com	(C) cloudfront .net	**(Y) google analytics .com**	(C) tmcdn.net	(D) googlesyn dication.com	(Y) google.com	**(Y) google analytics .com**
(O) facebook .com	**(Y) google analytics .com**	(C) cloudfront .net	(Y) baidustatic .com	**(D) double click.net**	(Y) histats.com	**(D) double click.net**
(Y) google analytics .com	(Y) google.com	(Y) google.com	**(Y) google analytics .com**	(Y) google.com	(D) 12mlbe .com	(Y) google.com
(D) adnxs.com	(O) facebook- .com	(D) googlesyn dication.com	(Y) cnzz.com	**(Y) google analytics .com**	(D) c21.ir	(D) googlesyn dication.com
(D) googlesyn dication.com	(O) twitter.com	(O) facebook .com	(C) taobaocdn .com	(O) facebook .com	**(D) double click.net**	(O) facebook .com
(D) scorecard research.com	(D) adnxs.com	(C) fbcdn.net	(G) 51seer.com	(O) twitter.com	(W) webgozar .ir	(O) twitter.com
(C) cloudfront .net	(C) fbcdn.net	(O) twitter.com	(T) sinajs.cn	(C) googleuser content.com	(R) dabi.ir	(P) anythumb .com
(O) twitter.com	(D) googlesyn dication.com	(D) adnxs.com	(S) ol- img.com	(P) anythumb .com	(Y) gstatic.com	(Y) gstatic.com
(D) 2mdn.net	(D) 2mdn.net	(D) betrad.com	(D) tanx.com	(Y) gstatic.com	(C) googleuser content.com	(D) adnxs.com
(T) amazonaws .com	(C) opta.net	(T) googleapis .com	(S) csbew.com	(T) googleapis .com	(P) anetwork.ir	(D) addthis .com
(Y) quantserve .com	(P) anythumb .com	(Y) gstatic.com	**(D) double click.net**	(C) cloudfront .net	(R) parset.com	(T) googleapis .com
(D) betrad.com	(D) scorecard research.com	(D) rubicon project.com	(W) hdslb.com	(D) addthis .com	(D) adnxs.com	(C) googleuser content.com
(P) anythumb .com	(T) googleapis .com	(D) scorecard research.com	(C) alicdn.com	(C) ytimg.com	(R) clipdooni.c	(C) cloudfront .net
(C) fbcdn.net	(T) amazonaws .com	(D) 2mdn.net	(A) allyes.com	(D) 2mdn.net	(T) googleapis .com	(C) phncdn .com
(T) googleapis .com	(D) betrad.com	(T) amazonaws .com	(R) qq.com	(D) zedo.com	(X) saba- e.com	(P) 220tube .com
(Y) chartbeat .net	(Y) quantserve .com	(D) googlead services.com	(N) jrjimg.cn	(D) adnxs.com	(C) cloudfront .net	(D) 2mdn.net
(D) newsinc .com	(D) googlead services.com	(Y) chartbeat .net	(V) letvimg .com	(D) betrad.com	(A) adsready .com	(D) adsafeprot ected.com
(D) yieldman ager.com	(T) brightcove .com	(Y) google.co .uk	(W) tuan800 .net	(C) phncdn.com	(A) enamad.ir	(D) scorecard research.com
(Y) gstatic.com	(Y) gstatic.com	(T) twimg.com	(C) babytree img.com	(P) 220tube .com	(A) ad2ad.ir	(C) ytimg.com

4   Related Work

A number of recent studies have explored modern web traffic, some of which specifically focused on analysing third-party trackers. Here we mention a few which are closely related to our work. Krishnamurthy & Wills [5] investigated the evolution of third-party trackers from 2005 to 2008. They identify the top-10 trackers using an approach based on the *adns* method. They had previously examined how different trackers work and collaborate with each other [7].

Roesner *et al.* [8] suggest a framework for classifying the behaviour of web trackers as well as showing the spread of the identified classes amongst top 500 websites in the world. Our work is closest to that done by Castelluccia *et al.* [9] which analyses the top 100 most popular sites worldwide across a number of countries to assess their tracker behaviours. Their work shows that despite heavy dominance of US-based websites across the visible and invisible web, some countries like China and Russia showing strong differences in local tracking behaviours.

All the above studies focus on specific types of third-party trackers on the web. A similar study was also carried out for mobile ads [10]. In contrast, our study examines the presence of all third-party websites among different sets of popular origin websites, when viewed from a single source.

Third-party websites, in the sense of any non-origin-site HTTP referral, have been studied by Butkiewicz *et al.* [4]. They categorise non-original sites based on the type of services they offer, and strongly inspired our categorisation (Table 1). They categorised the top 200 trackers using regular expressions and automated lookups; in contrast, we categorised about 600 third-party websites, also partly relying on manual inspection.

Ihm & Pai [11] report a longitudinal analysis on web tracking technological advances in various countries from 2011. They focus on the technology rather than providing detailed information on top individual ad-trackers per country. They find that ad traffic has been increasing, although they don't identify ad domains.

These studies attempt to explain the mechanisms of web trackers and their prevalence in today's Internet. In contrast, in this paper we have compared the presence of web-trackers across different countries and common language regions.

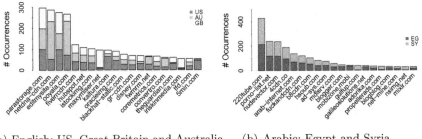

(a) English: US, Great Britain and Australia.   (b) Arabic: Egypt and Syria.

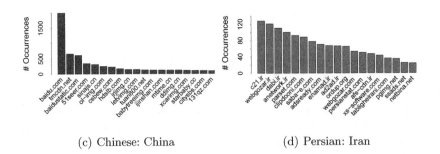

(c) Chinese: China   (d) Persian: Iran

Fig. 5. The top 20 third-party websites which appear exclusively in a specific group of countries

5   Conclusions and Future Work

In this paper, we studied the presence and use of so-called third-party websites on the web. We sampled every continent, targeting the 500 most popular websites in the US, Great Britain, Australia, China, Egypt, Iran and Syria. We examined this data by country and by grouping countries with a common language. Perhaps unsurprisingly, our results show that Google properties dominate overall, occupying four of the top five positions, and eight of the top 20. Two specific Google properties sites, DoubleClick and Google Analytics, are the only ones that are in the top 20 in every country we examined.

Cultural/language effects are also significant, with a great deal of similarity between the top 20 lists and referrals for the three western English speaking countries (US, Great Britain, Australia), and between the two Arabic countries (Egypt, Syria), and notable differences between those each of the four language groups (English and Arabic plus the two singleton groups, Persian/Iran and Chinese/China). Google properties, and ad tracking and tracking sites generally dominate everywhere. There are also minor differences in the prevalence of categories in the different countries: web hosting, portals and advertising only appeared in Iran and China, and porn was slightly more prevalent in the Arabic countries (Egypt, Syria). Further analysis on the effect of language and culture, however, requires bigger groups of countries. For example in our dataset, the Chinese and Persian speaking groups each contained only one country but those languages are also spoken in several other countries. The English speaking group can be also expanded to contain other countries such as India which is culturally different from other countries in this group. Additionally, in our measurements we monitor those third-party websites which are visible through our single vantage point while monitoring the popular websites from a different vantage point (e.g., different countries) may reveal different third-party services. We plan to address these limitations in our follow-up studies of the personal data ecosystem.

Acknowledgements. This work was funded in part by Horizon Digital Economy Research, RCUK grant EP/G065802/1.

References

1. Crane, D., Pascarello, E., James, D.: Ajax in Action. Manning Publications Co., Greenwich (2005)
2. Popa, L., Ghodsi, A., Stoica, I.: HTTP as the narrow waist of the future internet. In: Proceedings of the 9th ACM SIGCOMM Workshop on Hot Topics in Networks (HotNets), pp. 6:1–6:6. ACM, New York (2010)
3. Labovitz, C., Iekel-Johnson, S., McPherson, D., Oberheide, J., Jahanian, F.: Internet inter-domain traffic. SIGCOMM Comput. Commun. Rev. 41(4) (August 2010)
4. Butkiewicz, M., Madhyastha, H.V., Sekar, V.: Understanding website complexity: measurements, metrics, and implications. In: Proceedings of the ACM SIGCOMM Internet Measurement Conference (IMC), pp. 313–328. ACM, New York (2011)

5. Krishnamurthy, B., Wills, C.: Privacy diffusion on the web: a longitudinal perspective. In: Proceedings of the 18th International Conference on World Wide Web (WWW), pp. 541–550. ACM, New York (2009)
6. Mortier, R., Haddadi, H., Henderson, T., McAuley, D., Crowcroft, J.: Challenges & opportunities in human-data interaction. In: DE 2013, Open Digital, MediaCityUK, Salford, UK (2013)
7. Krishnamurthy, B., Wills, C.E.: Generating a privacy footprint on the Internet. In: Proceedings of the 6th ACM SIGCOMM Conference on Internet Measurement, IMC 2006, pp. 65–70. ACM, New York (2006)
8. Roesner, F., Kohno, T., Wetherall, D.: Detecting and defending against third-party tracking on the web. In: USENIX Symposium on Networking Systems Design and Implementation (NSDI) USENIX (2012)
9. Castellucia, C., Grumbach, S., Olejnik, L.: Data Harvesting 2.0: from the Visible to the Invisible Web. In: The 12th Workshop on the Economics of Information Security, Washington, DC, USA (June 2013)
10. Vallina-Rodriguez, N., Shah, J., Finamore, A., Grunenberger, Y., Papagiannaki, K., Haddadi, H., Crowcroft, J.: Breaking for commercials: characterizing mobile advertising. In: Proceedings of the ACM Internet Measurement Conference, IMC (2012)
11. Ihm, S., Pai, V.S.: Towards understanding modern web traffic. In: Proceedings of the ACM SIGCOMM Internet Measurement Conference, IMC (2011)

Peeking through
the BitTorrent Seedbox Hosting Ecosystem

Dario Rossi[1,2], Guilhem Pujol[2], Xiao Wang[2], and Fabien Mathieu[3]

[1] Telecom ParisTech, Paris, France
`dario.rossi@enst.fr`
[2] Ecole Polytecnique, Paris, France
`first.last@polytechnique.edu`
[3] Alcatel Lucent Bell Labs, Paris, France
`fabien.mathieu@alcatel-lucent.com`

Abstract. In this paper, we propose a lightweight method for detecting and classifying BitTorrent content providers with a minimal amount of resources. While heavy methodologies are typically used (which require long term observation and data exchange with peers of the swarm and/or a semantic analysis of torrent websites), we instead argue that such complexity can be avoided by analyzing the correlations between peers and torrents. We apply our methodology to study over 50K torrents injected in ThePirateBay during one month, collecting more than 400K IPs addresses. Shortly, we find that exploiting the correlations not only enhances the classification accuracy keeping the technique lightweight (our methodology reliably identifies about 150 seedboxes), but also uncovers seeding behaviors that were not previously noticed (e.g., as multi-port and multi-host seeding). Finally, we correlate the popularity of seedbox hosting in our dataset to criteria (e.g., cost, storage space, Web popularity) that can bias the selection process of BitTorrent content providers.

1 Introduction

Being one of the most successful P2P applications, BitTorrent has been dissected under many angles, from focused performance analysis to broad studies of the whole ecosystem. The present work focuses on the identification and characterization of the peers that inject content in P2P systems. A simple method consists in joining a swarm just after it has been advertised on a torrent website, in the hope that the monitoring peer finds the swarm populated with one unique seeder. However, this method fails when multiple peers are found, e.g., due to the injection of fake IPs or the use of multiple initial seeders. In such cases, heavier methodologies are usually used, which require long term observation and data exchange with peers of the swarm and/or a semantic analysis of torrent websites. These techniques require the exchange of significant amounts of data (see Sec. 2 for details). We instead advocate a lightweight technique that exploits multiple sources of correlations between peers and swarms (see Sec. 3).

Obvious tensions exist between BitTorrent users, content copyright holders and government agencies – recent studies indicate an increased uptake in the use of foreign seedboxes to bypass local jurisdictions [1]. Following the authors of [2, 3], we do not

A. Dainotti, A. Mahanti, and S. Uhlig (Eds.): TMA 2014, LNCS 8406, pp. 115–126, 2014.

take sides in this struggle. Detecting the content provider can be used for multiple purposes: torrent Websites could automatically detect producers of sensitive, unsolicited or non-compliant content, making it more efficient to remove content and accounts (which indeed happens but at a relatively long timescale [4], suggesting humans are in the loop); governmental agencies could use similar techniques to narrow down the list of potential suspects, thereby reducing the risk of generating false alarms (i.e., targeting users printer and WiFi access point as in [2]).

This paper makes a number of contributions. We develop a lightweight methodology exploiting multiple sources of correlation (Sec. 3), pinpointing a small number of peers (4K) responsible for a large fraction of content (60%). We confirm that our methodology correctly identifies seedboxes by performing reverse DNS lookups and extensive manual verification: we can associate about 150 peers, responsible for about 40% of all torrents, to known seedbox services (Sec. 4). Our methodology also exposes two interesting, yet previously unnoticed, seeding behaviors:

- seedboxes using multiple ports for the same IP address (that others have generally considered to be multiple peers behind a NAT box [4, 5]);
- groups of heterogeneous seedboxes (e.g., using different IPs, hosting providers, ASs), that consistently seed the same set of torrents, and that are thus managed by a single BitTorrent content provider.

We then estimate the seeding cost incurred by BitTorrent content providers, and correlate the popularity of seedbox hosting in our dataset to criteria (e.g., cost, storage space, Web popularity) that can bias their selection (Sec. 5). Finally, we conclude the paper outlining also future directions (Sec. 6).

2   Related Work

The study of alleged content providers in BitTorrent started with the seminal work of Piatek et al. [2], in turn a byproduct of another work from the same authors [3]: while studying BitTorrent performance in the wild, they managed to attract a number of (false positive) Digital Millennium Copyright Acts (DMCA) takedown notices. Authors showed that simple techniques may implicate arbitrary network endpoints in illegal content sharing (e.g., as a tracker may let peers specify an arbitrary IP in their announce), effectively managing to frame printers and wireless APs into getting DMCA notices. Since the study of BitTorrent requires some active crawling, authors seldom provide a broad view of the ecosystem [6], usually preferring to focus on some specific aspect [2–5, 7–11].

We report a brief summary of the closest work to ours in Tab. 1. As just said, [2, 3] focus on DMCA notices. Authors in [8] are interested in application- and network-layer heuristics to find clients with deviant behaviors (e.g., monitoring peers) to possibly construct blacklists on-the-fly to enforce user privacy. Authors in [4, 11], classify content providers in fake, profit-driven and altruistic categories. Both work agree that roughly half of the top-100 producers are profit-driven [4, 11], and [11] further points out that fake publishers are dominant among the top-861 producers, which are responsible for an estimated 60% of the total downloaded BitTorrent content. Hence, effective filtering

Table 1. Comparison of Related Work

Ref	Year	Duration	Torrents	Peers	Focus
[3]	2007	30 days	55K	-	DMCA notice
[2]	2008	30 days	27K	-	DMCA notice
[8]	2009	45 days	top 600	37M	240 deviant clients
[5]	2009	48 days	39K	148M	top 10,000 users
[4]	2010	80 days	55K	35M	top 100 publisher (37% of content)
[11]	2011	38 days	52K	16M	top 861 publisher (67% content)
this work	*2013*	*37 days*	*57K*	*443K*	*150 seedboxes*

of fake publishers could reduce network resource waste. Finally, [5] provides heuristics to classify the user type (e.g., proxy, Tor, monitors) while [10] does so by using PageRank-like algorithms on the user-content graph.

The above work generally relies on direct data exchanges with discovered peers, to verify that they actually own copies of the content (as otherwise the problems noticed in [2] may appear). Such resource-consuming approaches are hard to avoid if one aims at studying with precision and certainty one given peer or one given swarm, but we advocate that a preliminary filtering may significantly reduce the amount of work needed. For example, by joining a swarm immediately after its torrent has been published, we significantly reduce the number of IPs collected to some 443K (as opposite to 10M-100M in other works). Also, we employ an aggressive filtering phase that reduces the false alarm rate to a minimum, thus pinpointing 150 seedboxes responsible for about 40% of the content. Direct techniques such as those proposed in [2,4,5,11] could then be used on this more reduced, and more interesting, producer subset.

The present work also differs from [2,4,5,11] by not relying on cross-checking with external sources (e.g., user ID in the PirateBay portal) as they can easily be gamed (e.g., a sybil attack creating multiple user IDs). Conversely, we argue that network level data is less easily modifiable and thus more reliable: for instance, frequent changes of IP address involve either non-trivial techniques as the use of botnets or IP forging through BGP hijacking (due to the necessity of receiving traffic), or negotiations with multiple hosting providers, which may be slow, costly and thus impractical (due to monthly service fees). Another important contribution of this work is to correlate multiple observations of individual torrents along several dimensions, which brings a significant improvement while maintaining a desired lightweight property. Additionally, by exploiting correlations, we expose previously unnoticed seeding behaviors, partly countering common wisdom [4,5].

A final, notable, contribution of this work beyond the state of the art is a systematic study of the BitTorrent *seedbox ecosystem*, which has been previously only hinted to by [4,7] but never thoroughly assessed. We point out that, for the time being, we are not interested in addressing whether the content is legitimate or fake. Our analysis of torrent seeding costs holds irrespectively of whether the costs have to be sustained by a producer of real torrents, or by a polluter of fake ones (though this could be easily extended as discussed next).

3   Classification Methodology

Our detection methodology works as follows: we collect data by periodically (every 10 seconds) scraping the "recent torrents" page `http://thepiratebay.se/recent` at ThePiratebay. The page, whose average size is 57KB, is parsed for new torrents[1]. As soon as a new torrent is added to the list, we fetch the torrent (35KB average) and connect to the tracker to get the peer list (1 UDP packet).

We then rely on heuristics, described in what follows, to classify the torrent producer. Since we are not interested in discriminating between real vs fake torrents, we avoid checking whether the torrent exists for several hours/days after it is first injected (since in case the torrent quickly disappears or is banned, this can be used as a reliable indication of fake torrents [4]), though this would be a natural next step.

3.1   Unique Seed (S)

In case the content that has been added to ThePirateBay (TPB) is genuinely new, then there are chances that the peer list is reduced to one *unique seed*. As done in previous work [4, 5, 8–11], this simple heuristic allows us to conclude that the seed is likely to be the content originator. Formally, whenever a peer (identified by an endpoint IP:port) matches this simple heuristic for a torrent, we label the peer (and the corresponding torrent) as "S".

However, there are multiple reasons why this heuristic may fail. First, peers may add a torrent to the ThePirateBay that is already published somewhere else, so that the tracker may return multiple peers/seeds ([6] reports this to be often the case for ThePirateBay). Second, content originators may use some strategies to disguise themselves, such as using (i) injecting fake IPs to the tracker, as exploited in [2]; (ii) purposely using multiple ports per IP, to trick monitors in believing the observed IP is that of a NAT box; (iii) using multiple distinct dedicated servers, known as *seedboxes*, per torrent.

Yet, while the "S" classification (*individual observation over single torrents*) may fail due to the above reasons, we argue that *multiple observations over several torrents* can leverage the wealth of additional information to identify the largest fraction of the above instances. More precisely, we propose to exploit correlation in (i) time, (ii) TCP/IP space and (iii) content.

3.2   Correlation in Time (T)

We use the classification "T" to denote a correlation in time between swarms. When the tracker returns a list with more than one seeder for a newly injected torrent, a single observation is not enough to isolate the actual content provider(s). However, if a peer that has been previously labeled "S" for another torrent belongs to this list, it is reasonable to assume this peer to be the original content provider of this torrent as well, following a label propagation approach usually done in the classification literature [12]. Notice that in this way we may find peers disguised among other nonexistent peers (e.g., due

---

[1] Alternatively, we could subscribe and parse the RSS feed on all new torrents
`rss.thepiratebay.se/0`

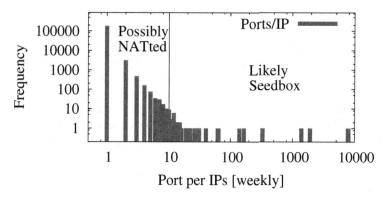

Fig. 1. Number of ports per IP (weekly observation interval)

to fake injected IPs) or among other legitimate peers (e.g., when torrents are added to ThePirateBay after being added to other torrent Website, thus after a swarm is already formed, as observed in [6]).

3.3 Correlation in the TCP/IP Space (P)

Let us then address the correlation in the TCP/IP space, and more precisely focus on the TCP port number (denoted as "P" in the following). It is typically considered that whenever multiple ports are observed for a single IP address, this is due to peers behind a NAT, so that the IP address observed is that of the NAT device [4, 5]. Additionally, authors in [5] notice that the number of ports grows proportionally to the number of torrents, suggesting that this is indeed due to multiple users downloading torrents with clients configured with different random ports.

We argue that while this reasoning is correct in most of the cases, some content providers purposely exploit this belief to disguise themselves. To support this argument, Fig. 1 shows the frequency of port number per peer in the typical week in our dataset. It can be seen that while in a large majority of cases, a single TCP port corresponds to a single IP, a number of endpoints deviate from this rule (likely due to NAT) and furthermore some endpoints exhibit *large* deviation (topping to almost 10000 ports behind the same IP). Based on Fig. 1, whenever we find that a newly injected content is seeded by peers with the same IP but different port, we label the torrent (and the IP) as "P".

3.4 Correlation in Content Space (C)

Finally, let us consider the correlation in the content space (denoted "C"), whereby we may observe multiple endpoints that are disjoint in the IP address space, but that are clustered in the content space.

A common practice in the content diffusion business consists in using multiple CDN services for resilience and performance (e.g., Netflix employs 3 CDN operators). It is reasonable to assume that similar good practices are adopted by professional Bit-Torrent content providers. Yet, in case BitTorrent content providers employ multiple seed-hosting services, endpoints will be totally unrelated in the IP address space[2]. However, in case such unrelated IPs systematically seed the same (or similar) groups of torrents, they can be easily clustered using typical Community of Interests (CoI) techniques. Of course, BitTorrent consumers can also exhibit some affinity and show a form of clusterization, but the content providers that use multiple seedboxes create communities that drift significantly from human behavior in terms of sizes: seedbox clusters are smaller (in terms of IPs) and much more correlated than human communities. Specifically, a group of torrents and peers is flagged as "C" when they are consistently observed seeding a group of at least C_{min} torrents. We tolerate slight differences in the set composition as the peer list may be partial or all seedboxes from a given cluster may not be active at the same time. This is managed by setting a threshold on a distance between peer lists.

More formally, we denote with $T(p)$ the set of torrents associated to a peer p. $J(p, q)$ is the Jaccard distance between peers $T(p)$ and $T(q)$, that is:

$$J(p,q) := 1 - \frac{|T(p) \cap T(q)|}{|T(p) \cup T(q)|}$$

The peers flagged "C" are selected as follows: we first restrict ourself to the peers p such that $|T(p)| \geq C_{min}$ for some C_{min}. We then select a maximal peer $p_0 = argmax_p |T(p)|$. If $B(p_0, \epsilon) := \{p : J(p, p_0) \leq \epsilon\}$ contains more than p_0, the whole set is classified as "C", along with corresponding torrents. Then $B(p_0, \epsilon)$ is discarded and we iterate the process.

Though the algorithm complexity may be quadratic in the number of torrents, practical complexity significantly reduces when the input is preliminary sorted by decreasing set size. Thanks to the parameter C_{min}, which we set to 5 based on preliminary tests, input size shrinks (57K to 1875) and so does the running time (2hr to 1min). We also set empirically the maximum Jaccard distance to $\epsilon = 1/C_{min}$ (i.e., 4/5 torrents in common). We point out that results qualitatively hold for other parameter settings, that we are however unable to fully report due to lack of space.

4   Classification Results

We apply the above heuristic in series to the whole dataset $\mathcal{D}$: we first apply the single-observation heuristic S to obtain a dataset of matching peers and torrent $\mathcal{S}$; we then apply the time-correlation heuristic T, gathering a $\mathcal{T}$ dataset made of a subset of peers from $\mathcal{S}$ and torrents not in $\mathcal{S}$. We next obtain $\mathcal{P}$ by applying the space-correlation heuristic P to $\mathcal{D} \backslash (\mathcal{S} \cup \mathcal{T})$ and finally obtain $\mathcal{C}$ applying C to $\mathcal{D} \backslash (\mathcal{S} \cup \mathcal{T} \cup \mathcal{P})$.

4.1   Ground Truth

To assess the quality of the classification, we perform a reverse DNS lookup of the IP addresses of the peers individuated as content originator. The most reliable way to

---

[2] Unless the provider is renting multiple seedboxes of the same hosting facility, so that IPs would share a common prefix. Yet, as correlation in the IP space only covers a subset of the cases we consider, we neglect it in the following.

assess whether a seed (peer) owns torrent data is to download all (some) data chunks and verify their MD5 signatures.

Our university policy forbids us to engage in direct exchange of illegal content via BitTorrent, for which reason we cannot join torrents as a means of verification (besides, the use of super-seeding techniques would possibly void the usefulness of checks based on meta-data).

Yet, we point out that this step is unnecessary in terms of our verification. Recall that we are more interested in detecting "seedboxes" (as opposite to detecting generic "seeds"): this is because the use of a seedbox is correlated with continuous and sustained seeding, typical of professional activities (as opposite to sporadic seeding activities).

We then manually inspect the reverse names to find known seedbox-hosting services (labeled as "sbx" in Tab. 2, see Sec. 5 for an excerpt of this list) or known ISP providers. We also browse the websites of seedbox-hosting and of (many previously unknown) ISP providers as an additional check. Finding Web pages explicitly offering seedbox services for monthly fees (that we study in more details later in the paper) completes the DNS ground truth, making it very reliable.

In corner cases, e.g., whenever the DNS fails to return any result (i.e., no PTR record), we label the peer as *unknown* ("unk" in Tab. 2). When we gather a DNS PTR record but cannot find any *explicit* evidence of seedbox-hosting services, we prefer a conservative approach and do not *not* label the peer as "sbx", even though we cannot find any *explicit* evidence of legitimate ISP and, rather, we do find some hint of suspicious activities (e.g., as13285.net, outo.asia). Otherwise stated, some of these unknown boxes may be actually seedboxes that are simply hard to confirm as such via DNS, but that are instead captured by the above heuristics.

Two further points are worth stressing. First, as in any classification study, result accuracy is bound to the quality of the ground truth. Our interest with this regard is not to precisely calibrate these heuristics with the available ground truth, which leads to the inevitable tradeoff between false alarms (legitimate users believed to be seedboxes) vs. false negatives (seedboxes that remain undetected). Rather, we aim at showing that exploiting correlation along different dimensions enables light-weight seedbox detection.

Second, it could be argued that, reverse DNS queries (ignoring for the time being manual Web page verification) could be used not only as a ground truth, but also as a classification technique (e.g., by means of simple pattern matching on the DNS name). Yet, we point out that this approach would be bound to failure, in that as soon as DNS names would be used to detect (and possibly block) seedboxes, a simple countermeasure would be to remove reverse DNS entries (or use domain names that bear no relationship to BitTorrent seeding).

4.2   Classification Performance

Results in terms of torrents, peers and torrent/peer are reported in Tab. 2 for each heuristic, as well as for their combination (boldface, STPC row). In line with previous results [4, 11], we gather that overall only 4K/430K peers are responsible for 35K/57K torrents; furthermore, about 150 seedboxes are responsible for about 40% of the content.

Table 2. BitTorrent provider detection performance

$\mathcal{X}$	Peers					Torrents					Torrents/peer				
	sbx	unk	$\|\mathcal{X}\|$	$\|\mathcal{X}\|/all$	$sbx/\|\mathcal{X}\|$	sbx	unk	$\|\mathcal{X}\|$	$\|\mathcal{X}\|/all$	$sbx/\|\mathcal{X}\|$	sbx	unk	$\|\mathcal{X}\|$	$\|\mathcal{X}\|/all$	$sbx/\|\mathcal{X}\|$
S	121	691	2941	0.66%	4%	4972	4525	14630	26%	34%	41.09	6.55	4.97	39	8
T	121	148	925	0.21%	13%	7207	4832	18355	32%	39%	44.75	32.65	19.84	154	3
P	5	0	85	0.02%	6%	467	0	572	1%	82%	93.40	0	6.73	52	14
C	17	25	125	0.03%	14%	1284	298	1875	3%	68%	75.53	11.92	15.00	116	5
STPC	143	716	3151	**0.71%**	**5%**	13930	9655	35432	**62%**	**39%**	97.41	13.48	11.24	**87**	**9**
All			443217					57081					0.13		

For any heuristic, we report its recall $|\mathcal{X}|/all$ and seedbox rate computed as $sbx/|\mathcal{X}|$, in terms of both peers and torrents. As for the number of torrents, we find that S accounts for 26% of the observations (less than in [5]), that temporal correlation T is able to explain an additional 32% of torrents while P and C account for a small percentage of torrents (1% and 3% respectively). Interestingly though, we see that the simplest S heuristic has the lowest true positive ratio, as only 34% of torrents can be reconducted to known seedbox via reverse DNS queries, while seed ratio is higher for the other heuristics $T=39\%$, $P=82\%$ and $C=68\%$.

4.3 Emerging Behaviors

Notably, the very high seed rate for the P heuristic suggests that the use of multiple ports is not uncommon practice in professional seedboxes, debunking a common myth. A possible reason for this behavior is that most seedbox services do not shape the uplink bandwidth among servers in the same rack (see Tab. 3 in Sec. 5 for details): as such, the use of multiple "virtual server" per seed opportunistically increases the amount of aggregate bandwidth that the seedbox is able to obtain (until the point at which the server CPU becomes a bottleneck due to the high number of concurrent applications running on the same physical core). We note that port usage can be either restricted to narrow ranges, or uniformly span a rather large port interval. We examplify such behavior in Fig. 2, where a single IP address is responsible for seeding 39 torrents (grouped by a token of their name in the picture) using over 4000 ports, in generally restricted ranges (unless for the AXXP token). As it clearly emerges from the picture, the IP appears to be running multiple seedboxes, that are likely managed and configured by different individuals (or organizations).

While the low-level details of the virtualization techniques used are not openly advertised by seedbox hosting services (see Sec. 5), available offers however range from managing custom full-blown virtual machines, to simply running pre-configured copies of popular BitTorrent software (e.g., ruTorrent, rtorrent) possibly employing container-based emulation techniques.

Additionally, we also find that 125 peers are organized in groups of 2.5 distinct seedboxes on average. We report a scatter plot of the number of common torrents seeded by different IPs in Fig. 3. To be conservative, let us neglect cases where we observe at most 10 torrents to be seeded by no more than 10 IPs (gray shaded region): still, two interesting areas of the plot emerges. In the top-left area (common case), small groups seed a high number of torrent: to point out some relevant example, one of such groups seeds over 300 torrents using 3 seedboxes (seedhost.eu, mshost.ws plus an unknown

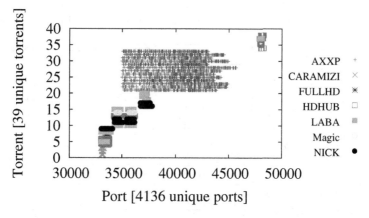

Fig. 2. Emerging behavior: multi-port seedboxes

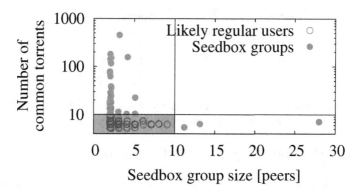

Fig. 3. Emerging behavior: seedbox groups

provider), while another group seeds over 100 torrents with 5 boxes (2 on kimsufi.com, 2 on novalayer.net and 1 on blazinseedboxes.com). In the bottom left area, rather large groups seed a smaller number of torrents (uncommon case): a closer look suggests one of such groups to be a monitor, whereas further investigation would be needed to better understand the structure of these fewer uncommon groups.

4.4 Significant Contributors

Finally, going back to Tab. 2, we see that the number of torrents seeded by each peer is significantly higher for seedboxes (40 to 90) than for other peers (5 to 20). Overall, peers matched by any of the S,T,C or P heuristic seed 87 times more torrents than the average peer (0.13 torrent/peer since multiple peers are possibly found per torrent). Furthermore, seedboxes seed 9 times more torrents than other peers in the S,T,C or P sets. Hence, peers exist that have quite serious commitments, requiring a significant amount of work (e.g., to package torrents, transfer them to multiple seed-hosting services, handling the contracts), as noted in [4]. While [4] focuses on prospective gains (e.g., distributing

Table 3. Seedbox hosting ecosystem: Popularity, Alexa Ranking and Service Features and Cost

Hosting Provider	Popularity			Alexa			Service: min vs. max storage, bandwidth and cost					
	T/P	T%	P%	Rank	Local	Indegree	minTB	minBW	minUSD	maxTB	maxBW	maxUSD
kimsufi.com	106.58	42.75	17.56	4610	437	2602	0.5	-	13	2	-	52
seed.st	41.44	16.38	17.3	136517	11540	787	0.1	2MBps	6	0.2	0.4TB/mo	40
novalayer.net	78.69	5.95	3.31	173014	0	13	0.2	-	15	4	-	141
nforce.nl	340.33	5.94	0.76	1.99E+07	0	399	0.2	1TB/mo	19.5	6	5TB/mo	221
xirvik.com	24.97	5.08	8.91	267295	170077	76	0.05	-	18	3	-	120
ovh.net	21.6	5.02	10.18	609	103	38844	4	-	90	8	-	117
leaseweb.nl	35.62	3.31	4.07	27388	2549	116	0.5	5TB/mo	39	4	100TB/mo	180
blazinseedboxes.com	35.54	2.69	3.31	958176	165834	34	0.2	-	15	8	-	150
voxility.net	51.43	2.09	1.78	72840	52522	47	-	-	-	-	-	-
seedmybox.com	24.77	1.87	3.31	221282	2126	205	0.3	-	30	1	-	57
leaseweb.com	20.21	1.65	3.56	3157	2642	1496	0.5	5TB/mo	39	4	100TB/mo	180
secureboxes.net	12.05	1.4	5.09	380643	18774	55	0.05	-	6	0.4	-	26
estroweb.in	17.5	1.22	3.05	5683848	0	7	0.12	-	19	0.5	-	49
aireservers.com	16.64	1.06	2.8	6010443	0	4	0.25	-	13	1	-	57
pulsedmedia.com	10.71	1.06	4.33	324688	9467	190	0.1	-	12	1	-	62

Table 4. Criteria for choice of seedbox hosting service

Pearson ρ	Alexa			Storage		Cost	
	Rank	Local	Indegree	min	max	min	max
T	-0.1	-0.1	0.0	0.0	-0.1	-0.2	-0.2
P	**-0.4**	-0.0	**0.3**	0.2	-0.2	0.0	**-0.4**
T/P	**0.8**	-0.2	-0.1	-0.1	**0.3**	-0.1	**0.5**

malware in case of fake torrents or advertising a website in case of real torrents), in the next section we reverse the perspective and quantify the cost they incur.

5   Characterization of Seedbox Hosting Service

We first report a detailed characterization of the seedbox-hosting ecosystem in Tab. 3, combining information coming from three sources. The first portion addresses the popularity of the hosting service in our dataset, reporting the percentage of peers $P\%$ and torrents $T\%$ employing each service, as well as the average amount of torrents seeded by peers as an indication of their relative level of activity. The second portion pertains to the popularity in the Web, reporting the global and local Alexa rank and the number of links pointing to the Website of the hosting service. The third portion reports the service SLA (i.e., storage space and bandwidth[3]) and cost (in USD) for low- vs high-end services, gathered by manually browsing the websites. Tab. 3 only reports the bulk of services accounting for 97.5% and 90% of the torrents and peers, and exclude a relatively long tail of unpopular hosting services. Notice that only a limited subset of hosting services that are popular in our trace appears to have been previously listed (e.g., in http://seedboxgui.de/). From the above dataset, we can extrapolate that the monthly operational expenditure (only considering the hosting service) of the 150 seedboxes observed during our study is about 33,000 USD – a rather tiny amount. While the average cost per seedbox is lower than 100 USD/mo, expenditure may be higher for providers using multiple boxes.

---

[3] Many hosting services only report Ethernet access (100Mbps/1Gbps), but the actual (unknown) uplink bandwidth will be shared among hosts.

Tab. 4 reports a correlation-based analysis of criteria for the choice of seedbox hosting service. We consider what criteria affect this choice by computing the correlation coefficient $\rho(X, Y)$ between pairs of vectors in Tab. 3. As for X we consider either the number of torrents T_s, peers P_s and T_s/P_s using a given seedbox hosting service s. As for Y, we consider the popularity of the hosting service in the Web (measured by Alexa rank, local rank or indegree), or the service features (minimum vs maximum storage space; we exclude the bandwidth for reason exposed above) and cost (minimum vs maximum cost). Mild (0.3-0.5) to strong (above 0.5) correlations are highlighted in boldface in the table.

Though unsurprising, two behaviors emerge from Tab. 4, which are mainly related with the size of the seeding business. First, considering the general seeding professional (row P), we can see that seedbox choice is biased towards popular hosting services that are also popular on the Web. Notice that a high Alexa rank (same for local) implies a low popularity for the hosting service in the Web, while a high Alexa indegree correlates with high popularity. Hence, the Pearson correlation coefficient has opposite meaning for these indexes: i.e, a negative (positive) correlation for Alexa rank (indegree) implies that popular hosting services used in the BitTorrent ecosystem are also popular on the Web. Furthermore, though peer choice is not correlated with the minimum service cost, high maximum cost may however be a deterrent for the average seeding professional $\rho(P, maxUSD) = -0.4$. As a consequence of these two facts, cheaper brands (i.e., kimsufi.com) of hosting services that are popular on the Web (i.e., OVH) are largely popular on the BitTorrent ecosystem as well (i.e., even though the kimsufi.com Website is not popular according to Alexa, the cheaper kimsufi offer is available from the OVH Website, which is instead highly popular).

Second, it is not hard to imagine that professionals seeding hundreds of torrents will have more stringent technical constraints (e.g., in terms of bandwidth or storage capacity). This is precisely what can be observed from row T/P, where choice is correlated to the ratio of the number of torrents seeded by peers: notice indeed the strongly negatively correlated with website popularity $\rho(T/P, Rank) = 0.8, \rho(T/P, Indegree) = -0.1$ but rather correlated with high-end performance and cost $\rho(T/P, maxUSD) = 0.5$. Specifically, few peers having the largest $T/P = 340$ ratio select one of the most costly providers (i.e., nforce.nl). Yet, cost reductions still matter even for professionals. For example, the seedgroup with the second highest average $T/P = 106$ ratio uses kimsufi.com to seed about 3 times less peers than those on nforce.nl. As the maximum cost on kimsufi.com is about 4 times less than on nforce.nl, this relationship is well captured by Pearson's correlation $\rho(T/P, maxUSD) = 0.5$.

We did not take into account additional factors that may bias hosting choice, such as *legal aspects* (e.g., countries more lax in fighting piracy may be preferred [1]), or *physical location* (e.g., seeding EU content from US or China may be inefficient; yet, this is unlikely as many Tab. 3 services offer users the choice of data-center location).

6   Conclusion

We propose a lightweight detection method of content providers in BitTorrent that exploit correlation in time, TCP/IP space and content. Analysis on a large dataset shows that the heuristic reliably detects seeding professionals. Notably, we uncover emerging trends of (i) groups of seedboxes hosted by multiple providers, and (ii) a systematic use of large ranges of TCP ports, that were both undetected by previous methodologies. Finally, we report a preliminary study of the cost incurred by BitTorrent providers, quantifying their operational expenditure for seedbox services. Despite novel insights, this work also leaves some interesting points unanswered. First, detection algorithm could be improved (e.g., by additional sources of correlation such as tokens in the torrent name) and fine-tuned (e.g., Jaccard threshold, using other distance metrics). Second, seedbox groups could be characterized from multiple angles (e.g., countries, AS). Third, metadata could be enriched (e.g., checking whether a torrent has been removed, correlating IP addresses with Spamhaus database).

Acknowledgement. This work started as a student project of the INF570 course at Ecole Polytechnique, was performed at LINCS http://www.lincs.fr, and received funding from the EU under the FP7 Grant Agreement n. 318627 (Integrated Project "mPlane").

References

1. Alcock, S., Nelson, R.: Measuring the Impact of the Copyright Amendment Act on Residential DSL Users. In: ACM IMC (2012)
2. Piatek, M., Kohno, T., Krishnamurthy, A.: Challenges and directions for monitoring P2P file sharing networks – or why my printer received a DMCA takedown notice. In: USENIX HotSec (2008)
3. Piatek, M., Isdal, T., Krishnamurthy, A., Anderson, T.: One hop reputations for peer to peer file sharing workloads. In: USENIX NSDI (2008)
4. Cuevas, R., Kryczka, M., Cuevas, A., Kaune, S., Guerrero, C., Rejaie, R.: Is content publishing in BitTorrent altruistic or profit-driven? In: ACM CoNEXT (2010)
5. Le Blond, S., Legout, A., Lefessant, F., Dabbous, W., Kaafar, M.A.: Spying the world from your laptop: identifying and profiling content providers and big downloaders in BitTorrent. In: USENIX Workshop on Large-Scale Exploits and Emergent Threats, LEET (2010)
6. Zhang, C., Dhungel, P., Wu, D., Ross, K.W.: Unraveling the BitTorrent ecosystem. IEEE Transactions on Parallel Distributed Systems 22, 1164–1177 (2011)
7. Han, J., Kim, S., Chung, T., Kwon, T., Kim, H., Choi, Y.: Bundling practice in BitTorrent: what, how, and why. In: ACM SIGMETRICS (2012)
8. Siganos, G., Pujol, J.M., Rodriguez, P.: Monitoring the bittorrent monitors: A bird's eye view. In: Moon, S.B., Teixeira, R., Uhlig, S. (eds.) PAM 2009. LNCS, vol. 5448, pp. 175–184. Springer, Heidelberg (2009)
9. Chen, X., Jiang, Y., Chu, X.: Measurements, analysis and modeling of private trackers. In: IEEE Peer-to-Peer, P2P (2010)
10. Avrachenkov, K., Goncalves, P., Legout, A., Sokol, M.: Classification of content and users in BitTorrent by semi-supervised learning methods. In: IEEE IWCMC (2012)
11. Kim, S., Han, J., Chung, T., Kim, H.-c., Kwon, T.'., Choi, Y.: Content publishing and downloading practice in bitTorrent. In: Bestak, R., Kencl, L., Li, L.E., Widmer, J., Yin, H. (eds.) NETWORKING 2012, Part II. LNCS, vol. 7290, pp. 97–110. Springer, Heidelberg (2012)
12. Zhu, X., Ghahramani, Z.: Learning from labeled and unlabeled data with label propagation. Tech. rep., CMU-CALD-02-107 (2002)

A Longitudinal Study of BGP MOAS Prefixes

Quentin Jacquemart[1], Guillaume Urvoy-Keller[2], and Ernst Biersack[1]

[1] Eurecom, Sophia Antipolis
[2] Univ. Nice Sophia Antipolis, CNRS, I3S, UMR 7271, 06900 Sophia Antipolis

Abstract. An IP prefix can be announced on the Internet from multiple end-points, possibly leading to so-called MOAS (Multiple-Origin AS) prefixes. Long-lived MOASes are traditionally considered to be the result of network topology engineering such as prefix multihoming. Short-lived MOAS are commonly attributed to be the result of router misconfigurations.

In this article, we look at MOAS prefixes in the long term and seek the patterns behind these situations. We first revisit previous work by looking at the duration of MOAS events. We group these events according to the prefix announced and show that short-lived MOASes are not due to misconfigurations, but to origin instability or route flapping. We also identify topology patterns that result in MOAS prefixes and use them to classify these events. We show that, contrary to popular belief, multihoming is neither the main use case leading to MOAS, nor the most popular pattern. Finally, we look at the evolution of these observations by analysing data collected 10 years apart.

1 Introduction

The Internet is composed of a set of interconnected independent networks, known as **Autonomous Systems** (ASes), that exchange reachability information containing **IP prefixes** through the use of **BGP** (Border Gateway Protocol). A MOAS event, MOAS prefix, or simply **MOAS** (Multiple-Origin AS) is the result of an IP prefix p being announced simultaneously from multiple endpoints. Even though RFC1930 [1] discourages MOAS situations, Zhao et al. presented a series of legitimate network engineering practices that lead to MOAS prefixes in [2], such as prefix multihoming and the use of anycast. These are expected to create **long-lived** MOAS events. Zhao et al.'s analysis also uncovered a number of **short-lived** MOAS events whose root causes are unclear, and were attributed to router misconfigurations. In this paper, we provide an in-depth study of MOASes with which we clarify and quantify the root causes behind long-lived and short-lived MOAS events.

First, we use a two-sided approach. By considering MOAS events individually, we revisit previous work by focusing on MOAS durations. Then, we provide the first study of MOAS events as groups of events related to their prefixes. With this study, we show that short-lived MOASes are less numerous than previously reported in [2]: many short-lived MOAS events are actually repeated events related to a small set of prefixes due to instability or route flapping.

Second, we introduce a taxonomy of MOASes into distinct MOAS patterns – **peering**, **classical**, and **me-too** MOAS – and study their prevalence and temporal characteristics. With these patterns, we show that the majority of MOASes are fake MOASes

A. Dainotti, A. Mahanti, and S. Uhlig (Eds.): TMA 2014, LNCS 8406, pp. 127–138, 2014.
© IFIP International Federation for Information Processing 2014

that are the result of loosely-defined, or outdated policies. The traditional MOAS shape only amounts to 30% of all cases.

Finally, we also look at the evolution of these findings by relying on the analysis of two full years of measurement collected 10 years apart, in 2002 and 2012 respectively, in order to underline discrepancies that may arise due to changes in standard practices, or due to the global evolution of the Internet.

2   Methodology and Dataset

2.1   Definitions

The Internet is composed of tens of thousands of interconnected independent **AS**es (Autonomous Systems). Inter-AS routing is done with BGP (Border Gateway Protocol), defined in RFC4271 [3]. BGP update messages are exchanged among BGP routers in order to propagate reachability information – containing IP prefixes and attributes – between ASes. One of these attributes is the **AS path**. When propagating a route, each router *prepends* its globally unique **ASN** (AS number) to the **AS path**. As a result, the *rightmost* ASN in the AS path is the **origin** of the route (unless the route was aggregated).

A **MOAS prefix** (Multiple-Origin AS) is the result of a prefix p being simultaneously originated from multiple ASes. In other words, at a given point in time, the AS paths for p end by a set $\mathcal{O}(p)$ of multiple origin ASNs, so that $\mathcal{O}(p) = \{a_1, \ldots, a_n\}$. For example, using Fig. 1, $\mathcal{O}_{]t_0,t_1[}(p) = \{1\}$, $\mathcal{O}_{]t_1,t_2[}(p) = \{1,2\}$, $\mathcal{O}_{]t_2,t_3[}(p) = \{2\}$, $\mathcal{O}_{]t_3,t_4[}(p) = \varnothing$, and so on. It is important to stress that MOASes only occur for the same prefix p. In particular, any prefix q more specific than p with a different origin than that of p is not defined as a MOAS prefix, but as a MOAS *sub*prefix (alternatively *sub*-MOAS), which we will not discuss in this document.

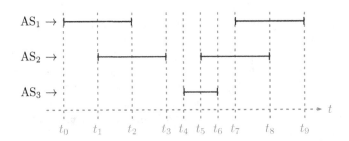

Fig. 1. Example of announcements for a prefix p

The literature defines **MOAS event duration** as the duration of a single MOAS event. In Fig. 1, the durations of the three MOAS events are $t_2 - t_1$, $t_6 - t_5$, and $t_8 - t_7$. MOASes are usually classified according to this metric with the following terminology [2]: **short-lived MOAS events** last less than 1 day, while **long-lived MOAS events** last more than 1 day.

If p is not a MOAS, but p is still present in the routing tables, p is a **SOAS** (Single-Origin AS), meaning that p is originated by a single AS. In Fig. 1, this happens during $]t_0, t_1[$, for example. If p is not included in the routing tables, we will say that p is **down** (Fig. 1 during $]t_3, t_4[$). This does not imply that traffic destined to p cannot be routed, because a set of covering prefixes could be used to forward the traffic. By contrast, a prefix is **up** whenever it is a SOAS or a MOAS.

We define the **lifetime** of a prefix p as the difference between the timestamp at which the prefix was last withdrawn (that is, the timestamp at which the prefix goes down for the last time) and the timestamp at which the prefix was first announced. The lifetime of p in Fig. 1 is simply $t_9 - t_0$. On the other hand, the **uptime** of p is defined as the total duration during which the prefix was advertised. In Fig. 1, the uptime of p is $t_3 - t_0 + t_9 - t_4$.

In Section 4.2, we introduce a new metric that we call the **MOAS duration per prefix** which is defined as the sum of the durations of the individual MOAS associated with this prefix. Using Fig. 1, the MOAS duration for prefix p is $t_2 - t_1 + t_6 - t_5 + t_8 - t_7$.

2.2 BGP Dataset

In order to study MOASes, we use data from RIPE RIS's [4] route collector located in Amsterdam (`rrc00`), which has above 40 geographically diverse peers. We retrieve the update messages and simulate BGP operations according to RFC4271 [3]. More precisely, we maintain a routing table for each peer – similar to BGP's Adj-RIB-In – the *adjacent routing table*. Each route announced by a peer is added to that peer's adjacent routing table. Whenever a withdrawal is received for a prefix, every route to that prefix is removed from the peer's adjacent routing table. Since we are not interested in routing traffic, we do not try to select preferred routes. We are, however, interested in knowing if a prefix p is up, i.e. if p is present in any of the adjacent routing tables.

The set of origins $\mathcal{O}(p)$ associated with prefix p is composed of the union of all the origins included in all of the AS paths of each adjacent routing table. If the cardinality of $\mathcal{O}(p)$ is larger than 1, p is a MOAS. For example, in Fig. 1, during $]t_0, t_1[$, $\mathcal{O}_{]t_0,t_1[} = \{1\}$ whose cardinality is 1, and the prefix is a SOAS. During $]t_1, t_2[$, $\mathcal{O}_{]t_1,t_2[}(p) = \{1, 2\}$ whose cardinality is 2, and the prefix is a MOAS. Finally, during $]t_3, t_4[$, $\mathcal{O}_{]t_3,t_4[}(p) = \varnothing$ whose cardinality is 0, and the prefix is down.

2.3 Methodology

Our study starts by revisiting the previous works [2, 5]: we compare the uptimes of MOAS and SOAS prefixes, and put into perspective the average uptime of MOAS prefixes with the average duration of MOAS events. By doing this, we show that our results are similar to what had been observed by [2, 5], thus ensuring that our further results can be put into perspective with the results provided by both of these studies.

We then consider that MOASes are not only a set of independent events, but they are related to a prefix. By grouping MOAS events per prefix, we are able to uncover inner relationships between multiple successive events. Most notably, we show that a large fraction of short-lived MOAS events are not the result of misconfigurations, which contradicts [2].

We look at topology graphs of MOAS prefixes from which we extract MOAS patterns that we use to classify and quantify MOASes. We study the temporal evolution of the topology graphs related to MOAS prefixes by comparing them months before and after MOAS events. This evolution enables us to understand the root causes behind the MOAS patterns.

3   Previous Work

Zhao et al. [2] pioneered the analysis of MOAS events, and analysed BGP data between late 1997 and mid 2001. This analysis concluded that 36% of the MOAS events were one-time events and lasted less than a day, 30% of which were attributed to a single misconfiguration. Excluding those, the average MOAS duration was 30.9 days. For MOASes that lasted over 9 days, the mean duration was 107.5d. These figures are computed using the MOAS duration per event.

The authors then discuss a number of reasons for which a prefix would be originated from multiple ASes: prefixes associated with an Internet exchange point (IXP) may be advertised by all the ASes within the IXP, since they are reachable through all of them. Multihoming without BGP (i.e. via static links or some IGP protocol) also leads to MOAS, since the prefixes are then announced by the upstream providers. Multihoming with BGP, but with a private ASN yields the same result. Anycasting can also lead to MOAS prefixes. Finally, since prefix aggregation in BGP transforms the AS path into an AS set (in which the order of ASNs is random), some artificial MOAS prefixes can be observed.

Chin [5] revisited the work of Zhao et al. by studying three weeks of data in January 2007, and found an average lifetime of MOAS events to be 13.25 hours. Chin then proposed new reasons behind MOAS prefixes: multinational companies may advertise prefixes from various branches in different countries, and such organizations possibly own multiple AS numbers. Companies may also host their servers in data centers, announcing the prefixes both, from the data center and from their offices.

Of course, MOAS prefixes can be the result of a malicious attack against the routing infrastructure, in which case they are often referred to as MOAS conflicts. As a result, the problem has been widely discussed in the literature related to prefix hijacking, such as [6, 7]. However these hijack papers usually focus on the threat posed by MOASes, not on their characteristics or classification.

4   Results

4.1   General Results

During the year of 2002, almost 310k different prefixes were announced, less than 9% of which presented (at least) one MOAS event. In 2012, there were almost 765k distinct announced prefixes, less than 6% of which were in a MOAS state at some point during the year. These figures suggest that, while both, the number of global prefixes and the number of MOAS prefixes increased in 10 years, their proportion has decreased.

Table 1. General statistics on BGP data for 2002 and 2012

		uptime			lifetime	
		μ	CoV	q_{50}	μ	CoV	q_{50}
MOAS	2002	328d	0.25	363d	334d	0.23	364d
	2012	308d	0.34	364d	317d	0.31	364d
SOAS	2002	146d	1.11	37d	172d	0.89	146d
	2012	223d	0.72	348d	239d	0.65	360d

Table 2. Duration of MOAS events

		μ	CoV	q_{50}
All MOAS events	2002	33d	2.23	22h
	2012	48d	1.88	26h
Short-lived MOAS events	2002	133mn	2.26	9.3mn
	2012	101mn	2.60	3.13mn

In both cases, less than 5% of MOAS prefixes were the result of route aggregations. We removed these prefixes from our MOAS cases before further analysis.

Table 1 shows the mean (μ), coefficient of variation (CoV = stdev / μ), and median (q_{50}) durations for the uptime and the lifetime of both MOAS and SOAS prefixes during 2002 and 2012. Mean values for MOAS prefixes in both, 2002 and 2012 are significantly higher than the values for SOAS prefix in terms of uptime and lifetime. This suggests the use of MOAS to improve the connectivity of a prefix. In particular, median uptime and lifetime of MOAS prefixes are both close to 1 year, meaning that 50% of those prefixes were seen over the entire observation period. The mean and median value for SOAS prefixes in 2012 – both close to 1 year – are also much higher than those in 2002, where the median uptime of 37d is very low compared to the observation period of 1 year, and to a median lifetime of 146d. These figures for 2002 are in line with the ones presented in [8], even though their analysis does not focus on MOASes, which strengthens our confidence in the accuracy of our method. While we only detail 2002 and 2012, we looked at the data of years in between and found similar conclusions.

MOAS Events. In this section, we consider MOAS events as a set of distinct events, independent of the prefix with which they are associated. For example, we consider independently the 3 MOAS events depicted in Fig. 1 during $]t_1, t_2[$, $]t_5, t_6[$, and $]t_7, t_8[$. The **MOAS duration** (per event) is the duration of a single event. In Fig. 1, the durations of the three MOASes are $t_2 - t_1$, $t_6 - t_5$, and $t_8 - t_7$.

Figure 2 depicts the duration of MOAS events in 2002 and in 2012. MOAS duration information for 2002 and 2012 are available in Table 2. The large difference between the mean and the median shows how prevalent short-duration events are. The consequence of the comparison between these values and those presented in Table 1 is that MOAS prefixes do not spend their whole life in a MOAS state.

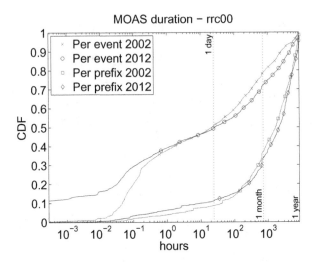

Fig. 2. MOAS events duration

MOAS Prefixes. In this section, we consider MOAS events grouped by the prefix for which they appeared. Distinct MOAS events may appear over the course of the observation period for a single prefix p. We say two MOAS events associated with a prefix p are **distinct** if the origin sets $\mathcal{O}(p)$ are different for the two events. For example, in Fig. 1, prefix p has 3 MOAS events: during $]t_1, t_2[$, $]t_5, t_6[$, and $]t_7, t_8[$. Moreover, $\mathcal{O}_{]t_1,t_2[}(p) = \mathcal{O}_{]t_7,t_8[}(p) \neq \mathcal{O}_{]t_5,t_6[}(p)$. So, even though Fig. 1 depicts 3 MOAS events, only 2 of them are distinct in the sense that they involve different ASes. Furthermore, the **duration** of **MOAS events per prefix** is the sum of the durations of the individual MOASes associated with this prefix. Using Fig. 1, the MOAS duration for prefix p is $t_2 - t_1 + t_6 - t_5 + t_8 - t_7$. In the remainder of this section, unless explicitly stated, duration means the duration of the MOAS events *per prefix*.

Figure 2 plots the duration of MOAS events per prefix. Only around 10% of the MOASes are short-lived, which heavily contrasts with the 50% obtained when considering each MOAS event on its own. This implies that certain prefixes must have many MOAS events. This is confirmed by Fig. 3, where the number of MOAS events and the number of distinct MOAS events per prefix are plotted[1]. The prefixes are sorted by decreasing number of MOAS events. For the first 1000 prefixes with the most MOAS events, the mean and median duration of single MOAS events is very small (in the order of a few minutes or less).

Figure 3 shows that, for approximately 1000 prefixes out of the 43k MOAS prefixes, the number of *distinct* MOASes is significantly lower than the number of MOAS events. Some of these prefixes only have 1 distinct MOAS, but hundreds of MOAS events. In these cases, there was a continuous flipping between SOAS and MOAS announcements. This kind of behaviour can be explained by an instability between the prefix owner and one of its upstreams. However, by looking at the AS paths in the duplicate BGP update

---

[1] The equivalent figure for 2002 looks very much alike, and was not included in the paper due to space restrictions.

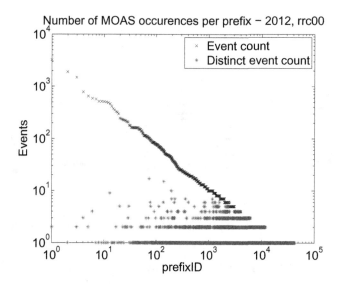

Fig. 3. Number of MOAS events per prefix

messages related to these events, we saw that only one sub-path actually caused this flipping phenomenon to the route collector. For this reason, we suspect that this flipping was not caused by an instability in the prefix owner's connections, but by some router located in an AS between the collector and the prefix origin.

Figure 2 also implies that the bulk of short-lived MOAS events *cannot* be attributed to misconfigurations. If, as supposed by [2, 5], most short-lived MOAS events are due to a misconfiguration, there should not be that many recurrent MOAS events for the same prefix. Indeed, only the sum of numerous short-lived events for the same prefixes (Fig. 3) can result in raising the MOAS duration per prefix as much, compared to the MOAS duration per event. Since misconfigurations are usually sorted out promptly [9], many short-lived events affecting many distinct prefixes would not shift the CDF plot to the right. As a result, the curves in Fig. 2 would not show such a drastic difference between the "per event" and the "per prefix" computations.

The mean and median MOAS durations per prefix in 2002 and 2012 are detailed in Table 3. We clearly see that both the mean and median values for the MOASes per prefix are a lot larger than individual MOAS event durations. This is, once again, the result of the combination of the many short-lived events per prefix.

We also considered the fraction of MOAS uptime for a prefix over its total uptime. One might expect MOAS prefixes to remain in MOAS state during most of their uptime in order to maximize the benefits behind their chosen MOAS configuration. However, the distribution of the fraction of time in MOAS state distribution is uniform and contradicts this expectation. We explain this phenomenon by the use of *transient* MOAS configurations. A temporal analysis of the topological evolution of MOAS networks uncovered multiple cases of stub networks switching between upstream AS providers. This operation can be summarized as follows. Originally, prefix p is announced by ISP A. At some point, the owners of p find it more advantageous to use ISP B. In order to

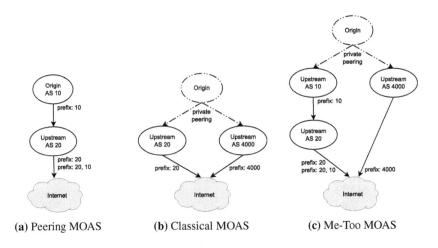

(a) Peering MOAS   (b) Classical MOAS   (c) Me-Too MOAS

Fig. 4. Graphs of MOAS patterns

avoid any service disruption, p remains connected to (and announced by) A while things are being set up with B (i.e. connecting p to B), and then also starting announcing it from B. This results in a MOAS. After some time (weeks), p is disconnected from A, and remains exclusively announced and reachable via B.

4.2 MOAS Patterns

We analyzed the AS-level graph of MOAS prefixes and were able to extract a set of patterns that result from MOAS announcements. This led us to a taxonomy of MOASes that we present now. In order to understand the reasons behind these MOAS events, we looked at the evolution of the AS topology of MOAS networks during 6 months surrounding the MOAS occurence.

The first pattern, depicted in Fig. 4a, shows a situation where both, the prefix owner and its upstream are announcing the prefix. We call this situation a **Peering MOAS**. Even though Fig. 4a only depicts one upstream, we saw cases where upstreams of the upstream were also announcing that prefix. The mean and median durations for peering MOASes are presented in Table 3. Figure 5 shows the distribution of the durations of peering MOASes for 2002 and 2012. 60% of those events last longer than a month, and around 10% of them are short-lived.

We often saw this pattern appearing in the following setting. The prefix is first announced by the upstream, but assigned to the customer (e.g. Fig. 1, during $]t_0, t_1[$). At some point, the customer decides to handle routing on its own, and acquires its own AS number and starts BGP peering with the upstream. At this point, there is a MOAS (Fig. 1, during $]t_1, t_2[$). Eventually, the upstream withdraws its announcement of the prefix, leaving only the owner's announcement in the routing tables (Fig. 1, during $]t_2, t_3[$). In this case, the MOAS was the side-effect of a real topology change. Even though we did not explicitly witness any situation in which this description is not accurate, this pattern is not necessarily the result of a provider-customer relationship. It is

Table 3. Duration of MOAS prefixes

		μ	CoV	q_{50}
All MOAS prefixes	**2002**	111d	1.01	71d
	2012	125d	0.95	90d
Peering **MOAS pattern**	**2002**	103d	1.03	64d
	2012	123d	0.97	88d
Classical MOAS **pattern**	**2002**	80d	1.24	32d
	2012	101d	1.12	43d
Me-Too MOAS **pattern**	**2002**	203d	0.64	241d
	2012	181d	0.60	197d

conceivable for this pattern to be the result of any direct peering relationship, such as peer-to-peer or siblings networks.

In other peering MOAS cases, the owner has several upstream providers, some of which re-announce the prefix. Effectively, the prefix owner is multihomed; but a subset of its upstreams originate the prefix. We believe that in this situation, the network was originally connected to a single upstream that handled BGP operations on its behalf, but then decided to multihome in order to benefit from increased connectivity. However, the original ISP's configuration remains unchanged and carries on announcing the prefix.

We consider this pattern to create **fake** MOASes because, in both of these situations, there is no gain for the owner from its upstream's announcement. Indeed, if the upstream stopped originating the prefix, the situation would remain unchanged: the prefix would still be reachable via all of its upstreams without loss of connectivity. Table 4 shows that peering MOASes amount to around 70% of all MOAS events. We believe this class of MOAS is caused by loosely-defined (or outdated) routing policy. Another cause would be prefixes associated with IXPs, as described by [2, 5].

The second pattern, depicted in Fig. 4b, is the expected AS pattern when talking about MOASes. For this reason, we call it the **classical MOAS** pattern. There are multiple distinct AS paths leading to the prefix. The mean duration of these MOASes are shown in the penultimate row of Table 3. These values suggest that classical MOASes are longer-lived in 2012 than in 2002. This is confirmed by Fig. 5 which plots the durations of these events. In 2002, around 50% of them were short-lived, which then decreased to around 35% for 2012.

We found the main reasons behind this pattern to be in accordance with engineering practices described in [2, 5]. In order to verify this, we used WHOIS data for the prefix and origin ASes. The ASes most often belonged to well-established ISPs, and the prefixes were registered to another entity. We also saw cases where multinational companies were the owner of each of the origin ASes.

Table 4 shows the proportion of classical MOASes among all MOASes, which is around 25%. Consequently, the pattern that is traditionally believed to be *the* MOAS configuration only amounts to a quarter of MOAS prefixes.

Any loss of origin in a classical MOAS means a loss of connectivity between the prefix and its upstream. If an origin AS stops announcing the prefix, it will not receive traffic for it. It will therefore not provide any connectivity to the Internet for the owner.

This contrasts with the situation of multihoming with a fake/peering MOAS, where the loss of an upstream origin does not affect the connectivity of the network, since the upstream AS remains in the AS path to the origin.

The last pattern, depicted in Fig. 4c, is named **Me-Too MOAS** to underline its "being over-announced" property. It is composed of both of the previous patterns at a single time: the left-hand side of Fig. 4c shows a peering MOAS, while the first-level AS peers are arranged in a classical MOAS manner. The mean and median durations of this pattern is shown in the last row of Table 3. These values suggest that me-too MOASes are stable. Figure 5 confirms that few of these events are short-lived (less than 5% in both cases), and over 80% of them last longer than two months.

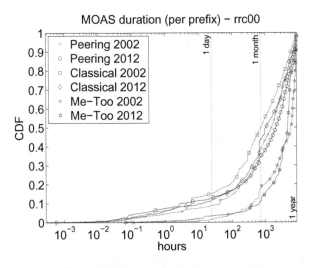

Fig. 5. MOAS patterns duration (per prefix)

We saw this pattern appear in the two following situations. The first one was a combination of subletting of IP space. Using Fig. 4c as illustration, the prefix block p is owned by AS20 and AS10 rents it. The WHOIS record associated with p clearly stated that prefix p was part of non-transferable IP addresses. So, because AS20 is the owner, it keeps on announcing p. However, since AS10 rents it, it also announces the prefix. This results in a peering MOAS, i.e. the left-hand side of Fig. 4c. Additionally, AS10 assigned p to one of their customer for use. At some point, this customer chooses to do multihoming and uses AS4000 for that purpose. In return, AS4000 announces p as well, i.e. the right-hand side of Fig. 4c. The second situation was when a prefix owner decided to change upstreams. Originally, the owner's prefix was announced by a tier-1 ISP which used multiple AS numbers, one for its global activities (AS20 in Fig. 4c), and one for its local activities (AS10 in Fig. 4c). However the ISP used both of those AS numbers to originate the prefix, although it needs to go through the local AS from the backbone to reach the customer (this corresponds to a peering MOAS). Then, the user (AS at the top of Fig. 4c) decides to switch their ISP service to another tier-3 ISP (AS4000 in Fig. 4c). During the transition, which usually lasts several weeks, the prefix

Table 4. Proportion of occurrences of MOAS patterns

Per prefix	2002	2012
Peering MOAS (a)	72.55%	72.63%
Classical MOAS (b)	31.09%	28.6%
Me-Too MOAS (c)	5.5%	3.84%
(a) & (b)	6.37%	3.24%
(a) & (c)	1.95%	1.59%
(b) & (c)	1.37%	0.49%
(a) & (b) & (c)	0.52%	0.24%

was announced by both the old tier-1 (AS10 and AS20 in Fig. 4c) and the new local tier-3 ISP (Fig. 4c, AS4000). This situation, then, presents a peering MOAS with a classical MOAS.

Table 4 shows that me-too MOAS events amount to 3% to 5% of MOASes. This can be explained by the fact that this configuration is unlikely to arise from erroneous situations, unlike the previous two patterns since it requires (at least) 3 origin ASes for a single prefix, *with* a peering relation among two of them.

The bottom rows of Table 4 show the proportion of prefixes that exhibit different types of MOAS patterns. These values suggest that MOAS prefixes only exhibit one kind of MOAS event throughout their lifetime. When we put this information in relation with the MOAS durations in Table 3 (125d on average) and the MOAS prefix uptime in Table 1 (308d on average), it is clear that MOAS prefixes do not spend their whole uptime in a MOAS state. However, the fact that the MOAS prefixes do not switch from one MOAS class to another suggests that their configuration remains stable. We can think of two main reasons why these MOAS announcements would be withdrawn. A reason could be that the owner of the prefix intentionally withdraws this announcement, for exemple due to exceeding the bandwidth allowance of one of its peer. Another reason is the data bias from our collector router, i.e. these routes are not propagated to the collector anymore because they have been filtered out.

5   Conclusion

In this paper, we studied MOAS events in multiple ways. First, we revisited previous works by looking at MOAS events on their own. Then we considered MOAS events along with their prefix. Grouping the events that way underlines the relationship between seemingly independent MOAS events. Most notably, we showed how many short-lived events repeat in order to result in a long-lived MOAS prefix. This observation eliminates the possibility that these events are the result of a misconfiguration.

We also looked at the evolution of the topology graph of MOAS prefixes and we classified MOASes into three distinct patterns. The most popular pattern, peering MOASes, is composed of long-lived MOASes where the different origin ASes are directly peering. We consider these as fake MOASes because there is no benefit from the MOAS announcement. The second class of MOAS is composed of classical MOASes. This is the standard MOAS configuration. However, they only make up for a third of the global

MOAS events and global MOAS prefixes. The last pattern, me-too pattern, is a combination of the other patterns and was encountered as a transitional configuration when an owner was switching its upstream provider to another one.

Finally, we looked at data ten years apart, and showed that there is little difference in MOAS properties in terms of prefix uptime, MOAS duration, and MOAS classification/proportion. This is remarkable because the size of the network grew by around 400% over this period of time [10].

Future work includes expanding our ground-truth sources with verified peering information to supplement WHOIS data. This would permit further validation and classification of peering MOASes. Another direction is to deeper study the flipping between SOAS and MOAS related to a single prefix. As we suggested, it may be the result of an intervention of the owner, in order to comply to the terms of a peering agreement (e.g. exceeded bandwidth). Finally, our analysis makes use of a single vantage point to analyse MOAS conflicts. This certainly results in under-estimating the number of MOAS events seen, particularly in terms of peering MOASes. (Classical MOASes try, by design, to diversify the AS paths as much as possible.) Although we are confident that the global trends and orders of magnitudes we exposed in this study remain true regardless of the vantage point, using (multiple) different route collectors would certainly provide better estimates.

References

1. Hawkinson, J., et al.: Guidelines for creation, selection, and registration of an Autonomous System (AS). RFC 1930 (March 1996)
2. Zhao, X., et al.: An analysis of BGP multiple origin AS (MOAS) conflicts. In: IMW (2001)
3. Rekhter, Y., et al.: A Border Gateway Protocol 4 (BGP-4). RFC 4271
4. RIPE NCC: Routing Information Service, http://www.ripe.net/ris/
5. Kwan-Wu, C.: On the characteristics of BGP multiple origin AS conflicts. In: ATNAC (2007)
6. Lad, M., et al.: PHAS: A Prefix Hijack Alert System. In: USENIX Security Symposium (2006)
7. Shi, X., et al.: Detecting prefix hijackings in the internet with argus. In: IMC (2012)
8. Siganos, G., et al.: BGP routing: A study at large time scale. In: Proc. IEEE Global Internet (2002)
9. Mahajan, R., et al.: Understanding bgp misconfiguration. SIGCOMM Comput. Commun. Rev. 32(4), 3–16 (2002)
10. Huston, G.: BGP reports, http://bgp.potaroo.net/

Author Index